On Foot to Machu Picchu

a duff trekker's guide

By Sharon McKee

dilliebooks

For Dylan

1 Preparations and panic stations

To visit Machupijchu, you must prepare the soul, sharpen the senses. Forget for some minutes, the small and transcendental problems of our lives, of modern... man..."

Napoleon Polo, Casilla 435 Cuzco Peru

The doctor entered the room without knocking. I got ready to answer his enquiries about my health but, instead, he said gruffly, "Your insurance company – no word from them." He then left the room. A tiny lady with a weather beaten face topped with jet black hair came in. She smiled a gap toothed smile and we exchanged 'Buenos dias'. She proceeded to clean the room, gloveless, using the same cloth to wipe everything from the toilet to the bedside cabinet, then departed with a cheery 'Adios'.

It was 8am on a Sunday morning in Cusco, Peru. I was in a hospital staffed by a Dr Dante and people who spoke little English. I vowed that if anyone asked how my 'holiday' was when I got back home I would hit them. This was by no stretch of the imagination a holiday.

***

It was a bleak wintery evening when an advert in a newspaper caught my eye and my imagination. There was a photograph of imposing jagged mountains standing guard around misty, mystical looking ruins. I was intrigued and tempted. I tore it out and kept wondering about it. I really wanted to go and experience it for myself. I pondered over that picture for days until I took the plunge and signed up to do a charity trek to Machu Picchu.

Immediately after I made the booking with a company called Charity Challenge, I wondered what on earth I was doing. I'd never even thought about doing anything like this before. Although I like exploring new places, I do like my home comforts - at least basics like toilets, running water, a bed. I have been camping just twice in my life - and never felt the urge to do it again. As for trekking up mountains, the nearest I get is walking the dog each day and meandering around hills in Northumberland. I usually sort out travel and holidays independently myself. The idea of being stuck in a group and having everything organised for you has never appealed.

I'd also never fund raised before – at least not since the annual sponsored walk at school many many moons ago. There were various options that I could sign up to with Charity Challenge, and I'd chosen one which committed me to raising at least £3,000 for Breast Cancer Care. As I'd been diagnosed with breast cancer three years earlier it was a chance for me to give something back and make a contribution to a charity that I'd personally had experience of and support from.

Finding the time between work, home life and everything else to fit in organising events, baking copious amounts of cakes, begging raffle prizes, thanking everyone kind enough to donate or help was definitely a challenge in itself. But the time finally came, after cake stalls, comedy nights, clothes swishes, and coffee mornings galore that met and actually exceeded the target. I'd raised nearly £4,000 for Breast Cancer Care. Now I could really focus on the next part of this challenge – the trek to Machu Picchu.

Charity Challenge, the organisation behind the trek, was able to put most of us who'd signed up to do this in touch with each other. Thankful for modern technology, we were scattered all round the country, and like me many of the others had signed up on their own. It turned out were an all female group and the initial polite introductory emails soon turned into girly questions, queries, planning and panicking. At first we were all focused on the fundraising – what worked, what didn't, companies that were supportive, events that flopped. Then as P Day, as departure day became known, fast approached we wondered about all the things it's probably difficult to get a grip of unless you've actually been. Just how cold would it be sleeping in a tent up the Andes, what was altitude sickness exactly, did we really need rabies jabs, how on earth did you use a Shewee, what if you had a period on the trek?

We exchanged so many questions and our replies and reassurances varied because, of course, none of us could really know what to expect. I discovered someone who lived near to me who had done the same trek with the same company the previous year so I met up with her.

It was, she said, "An amazing, incredible experience but absolutely exhausting. You're constantly on the go, you don't get any time to relax and no time to yourself." One of her concerns had echoed mine - how would I cope being with a group of strangers for 24 hours a day. Reassuringly she said her group bonded and supported each other, everyone had good days and difficult bits. She had suffered what became known as the Inca Two Step while out on the mountains and warned me, "You just have to hang behind, make sure everyone is ahead of you and go. Make sure you always carry tissues and a nappy sack." There was apparently not even a handy bush or rock to hide behind let along anything resembling a toilet. Would she do it again? "Absolutely."

I became a little obsessed about toilets, tiredness and training. Toilets, or rather the lack of, I could do very little about, except pack lots of tissues and wet wipes. Tiredness I could also do little about but had stopped taking medication that tended to give me insomnia and wipe out my energy. Fitness was one thing I reckoned I could work on. I went running three times a week and took the dog for long hill walks whenever possible. I paid for the pleasure of being shouted at twice a week in the gym by a personal trainer fondly nicknamed Scary Shaz. I had never exercised so much in my life and was toned like never before, causing my son Dylan to remark,"You look a bit butch mum." I conceded I'd maybe overdone the biceps a bit.

Occasionally described as a bit of a control freak (I prefer to say 'a good organiser') I'm used to being in charge at home and work. In recent years as well as horse riding and scuba diving on a favourite Greek island, holidays had included various city breaks, a trip to Russia, backpacking to Prague, Budapest and Vienna. The one consistent thing was arranging it all myself - the travel, accommodation, routes and lists of must sees and dos. I've never before been on an all organised for you group tour of anywhere. So not having to do the research or planning felt a little odd. I suddenly realised a few weeks before P Day that I hadn't even bought a guide book. Browsing in bookshops aiming to rectify this, made me realise just how little of this very varied country I'd be experiencing. It was difficult to find a book that didn't cover the whole of Peru and have only one out of perhaps 20 chapters relevant to this trip. I finally found one that was just about the area we'd be visiting - 'Cuzco and the Inca Heartland'. It recommended 'three or four weeks would allow you to enjoy the region to the full'. I was going to be there for a week.

Our starting point was to be Cusco, the 'gringo capital' of South America. Cusco was at the heart of the Inca Empire, today it's a mix of this ancient past, Spanish colonialism and now a backpackers must see. Cusco would also be our introduction to high altitude, located up in the Andes at around 3,400 m (11,200 ft) above sea level.

Our end point was of course Machu Picchu. Over 500 years old, it remained hidden until 1911 when the American Hiram Bingham chanced across it when he was actually looking for something else (the lost city of Vicabamba). Although hidden and inaccessible, the 'lost' city of Machu Picchu was actually pretty well known to locals who took him there. The intrepid explorer claimed the glory of 'discovering' it but it took 50 years before it was recognised as Machu Picchu.

I read through the final instructions and information pack from Charity Challenge. We were trekking along a route called the Lares Valley rather than the traditional Inca Trail that most people use. This one is now falling victim to its popularity and numbers allowed to trek along it are restricted and controlled. An alternative trail, our four day trek was to be along a much quieter and more remote route. I could find little else out about it.

As I re-read the itinerary I pondered how I was going to fit in a trip to the Chocolate Museum in Cusco, or a quiet cocktail at the little boutique hotel I'd seen online, let alone time for just sitting around taking in the sights and sounds. When we arrived in Cusco it would be about lunchtime and once checked in a guided walk around the city was the first thing on the itinerary, followed by a briefing, then dinner. Everything after that was listed in the same way - every day and hour seemingly accounted for. It was a packed itinerary from getting there to leaving. The lack of free time and time on my own would be another challenge. The distance it stated we walked each day didn't seem particularly long but I'd already been warned it was the high altitude that made it unexpectedly difficult. The lack of oxygen meant you have to go much slower than a normal pace. It was also pointed out that a good deal of the trek would be going upwards.

As P Day grew nearer the Peru posse's email debates intensified: how many packets of wet wipes to take (one may not be enough, three too many); whether or not to take water purifying tablets (the information reassured us that there'd be clean drinking water, but you never know); who was going to get their nails done before going (myself and several others). Bags were being packed and weighed, results shared in email conversations 'Just a bit over - do you think it'll matter?'... 'Going to wear my hiking boots on the plane can't fit them in'... 'Surprised I'm below the weight limit someone can have my spare'.

One week before we were due to leave an email arrived from the organisers. It informed us that there was going to be a Spanish airline strike which affected our flights - and as it stood they were now cancelled. It was like lighting a touch paper. We received the email late on the Thursday afternoon before Easter weekend. Friday and Monday were bank holidays. Offices were closed and there was nothing we could do except wait until Tuesday. I stopped looking at the frantic messages filling my inbox as I realised we'd just have to wait until we heard from the organisers after the weekend. Sure enough by Tuesday lunchtime we had news we were booked on alternative flights. Even the times were about the same so we could still get all our connections.

After that last minute panic and a frantic few days with little sleep, I was peeling my eyelids open in a taxi at 6am on P Day. Dylan came with me to see me off. It was the last of his display of support which had included donating a substantial amount of money and reminding me not to be 'too embarrassing' when I was fund raising. I checked in then we sat having a coffee in Starbucks, playing 'spot the other trekker'. There was one other person also travelling from Newcastle and we were meeting for the first time at the airport. I knew very little about her except that from the pictures on Facebook she looked very young and glamourous. I already felt frumpy in yoga pants and baggy t-shirt - I'd definitely gone for comfort over style for the long journey.

We passed the time having the type of conversation I could only have with with my teenage son.

"So if you do die when you're away, do I get the house and loads of money? You have made a will?" he asked, I think only half joking.

"I have more chance of being run over by a bus here. Nothing will happen to me. You'd better be careful too when I'm away, I'll hear everything from Googs and Grandad."

We hugged harder than usual before I left him to head through security. I love travelling with him and wished he was coming with me. I wanted to be sharing this adventure with my son rather than strangers. I turned round and watched him disappear down the escalator. I was on my own. I was off.

2 First Impressions

'There are no strangers here; only friends you haven't yet met' -
William Butler Yeats

One very organised member of the group, Jo, had suggested getting
together for a weekend away to go on training walks and meet up a
couple of months before we left. After email debates about dates
and location six of us had signed up for a weekend in the Peak
District. Finding a remote youth hostel in the middle of nowhere in
torrential rain and darkness at least helped break the ice, as we
shared tales of our treacherous journeys on arrival.

It was the first time we'd met but sharing one bunk bedded
room that smelt of teenage boys, giggling over drinking illicit wine
in our beds, quickly helped us bond. I was relieved to have met
them, it helped reduce some of my concern about being with a group
of strangers constantly for a ten days. That weekend the Peak Posse
as we called our small gang walked up the steep peaks, through
downpours, hailstones, gale force winds, supported each other and
laughed a lot. We got on so well it felt like we'd known each other
for ages.

It also helped alleviate some of the other concerns I had. We
all had different levels of fitness and stuck together as a group.
Although tired at the end of a day's walking I felt that my training
seemed to be paying off and it gave me confidence that I could do it.
In the Peak Posse, Suzanne and Andrea were already friends and by

the end of the weekend I'd paired up with Rose to be room/tent buddies, and Michelle and Jo did the same. Another concern ticked off.

When we said goodbye on the Sunday it seemed odd that the next time we'd see each other would be in Heathrow, when we were on our way to Peru. Those last couple of months flew by until somehow, suddenly, scarily, P Day had arrived.

Up until a few weeks before we departed, I thought I was the only one flying to Heathrow from Newcastle. I decided this would be good preparation time to try and get my head together for whatever lay ahead - and have the last bit of solitude for a while. But late in the day another girl from the area had signed up, so I was now meeting Mel for the first time at Newcastle airport. I didn't feel like I knew too much about her, though we'd linked up on Facebook, she hadn't been as prolific as some of us via emails. After I left Dylan I headed through security and sat with a coffee answering his texts of 'have you found her yet'.

When I did see her coming through the cafe she was quite easy to spot, the only person wearing a bright pink Breast Cancer Care t-shirt - of course. I waved, conscious that my dark blue top didn't help in the spot the trekker competition. She was as glamorous as she looked in her photos even wearing the charity t-shirt and hiking boots We chatted until it was time to board the plane with introductory conversations we were to repeat several times over about reasons for doing this, our family, jobs, fears.

Having deliberately got an early flight in case of delays, we arrived in London well before everyone else. With bags piled on a trolley we wandered around, realising we were in a really small part of the terminal with only a couple of shops and bars. We decided to settle in a bar with a large PUB sign and sat near the entrance reckoning it was an easy to see meeting place. Polite and pacing ourselves we opted for soft drinks until the others arrived. After an hour or so they did in ones and twos, and as the group grew we took over the whole area. Huge rucksacks covered the floor and chairs, there was a flurry of pink t-shirts and the sound of glasses of fizz being clinked.

As people turned up, I was putting names to faces and happy to be reunited with the Peak posse. The noise levels rose to the decibels a group of 15 quite excited women can make, as introductions were made and several different conversations took place at the same time.

By the time we were on our 3rd or 4th celebratory drink a clipboard wielding rep, who had been sent to see us off, appeared. Stern faced, she told us she had been looking all over for us and as we quietened like naughty school children she passed each of us large brown envelopes with our tickets, itinerary and a Charity Challenge T-shirt. Getting all of our bags and everyone together took some time but eventually we were herded through to check in, the relief on the rep's face was obvious - her job was done. Well, nearly.

There were actually two of the group missing. Suzanne and Andrea had had train cancellations scuppering their plans to get there from Manchester. They had texted to say they were jumping on a plane instead. The rep she assured us she'd do everything she could to make sure they'd get our plane - if not they'd be on the next one.

When we finally boarded the plane and were sitting in our seats, two pink t-shirted and pink faced figures dashed into the aisle - Suzanne and Andrea had made it. A loud cheer went up and now we really were heading off.

With everything on time we had a couple of hours to wait in Madrid airport to get the next connection. The ones who had planned well and brought Euros kindly shared them with us slightly less well organised ones. The longest flight was next, from Madrid to Lima and was overnight. By then though I was feeling tired I knew I'd be unlikely to sleep on the plane. Even a glass of wine with my bland airline dinner of rice and a couple of vegetables didn't help. But finally, after an unsettled few hours, the blinds were opened, light streamed in and everyone else was awake too.

We caught our first sight of Peru, flying low enough to identify mountains, beaches, and then high rises becoming visible as we went down to land at Lima. Another stamp added as we went through immigration, with only a slight delay as Jo was held up and questioned at the counter - for no obvious reason. At this point we had to collect our baggage and check in again to an internal flight to Cusco.

Having made it all the way on our own we were being met by a rep. But we were actually just literally met, greetings were polite but rushed. She counted us, possibly in case we'd lost anyone and not realised, then we were herded into the next queue and she waved goodbye as we went through security once again. We sat, working out time differences, it was something like 10am in Peru so about 4pm back home - I'd set off the previous day at 6am. No wonder even before I'd worked out when I last slept, I was feeling tired.

The plane to Cusco was a tiny aircraft but complete with complimentary snacks and that iconic image of Machu Picchu on the screens in between the seats. There were a lot of young people, flap eared hats and rucksacks - this was trekkers travel. "What is that?" a young lad next to me asked in a South African accent as the steward passed me a bottle of bright, urine coloured liquid. "Inca Kola," I said, showing him the label. "I have no idea what it's like but when in Peru.." "Oh, same for me then please," he said. We chatted as we had our first taste of the national fizzy drink that's nothing like Cola, and is so sweet you can positively feel the sugar eating into your teeth enamel.

Cusco is the capital city of the region, with around 1.5 million visitors each year. The airport, which acts as both the domestic and international airport, only operates during daylight hours. Here was my first lesson in adjusting to this experience - expect things to be basic - and basic to be less than normal basic. Walking through the tiny, old building to collect our bags we speculated about whether it was unfinished, under repair, or just was this way. Looking around we decided that it probably 'just was'. A much needed trip to the toilets also gave us our first taste of what to expect in the bathroom department. The fact that there was no toilet paper and no toilet seats were the least of the problems - there were no lights and no ceiling either. Welcome to Cusco.

The rest of the airport didn't fare much better. The baggage carousel (there was only one) came in to the one room near the entrance through a hole that looked hastily knocked out of the wall, you could see outside through it and watch the bags being thrown on. In the small crowded area we were approached by a number of smiling touts claiming to be taxi drivers and guides, before two men introduced themselves as being from the trek company and showed us their id. They filled a trolley each with our precariously piled up rucksacks and we walked out, past a stand selling oxygen in small bottles. It seemed a very odd thing to have and we joked about having to pay for fresh air in Peru.

Outside, standing by a coach a smiling, silver haired man introduced himself as Tony, our guide for the trip. He looked tanned, wiry and athletic, a little like a mature Action Man. Once we'd all climbed on board he introduced the driver whose name I instantly forgot and told us things about the itinerary that I also instantly forgot. I put my lack of focus down to sleep deprivation and 36 hours traveling.

The short bus ride took us through what looked like outskirts of a city, satellite dishes dotted about, an increasing number of buildings - yet it wasn't that city like at all. It wasn't built up, the buildings looked old, they were built low and scattered rather than tightly packed and mountains weren't just visible but seemed to be part of the cityscape, some with advertising hoardings on them.

The bus slowed, bumping over cobble stones and pulled up in a square. With no obvious signs of a hotel, we were led carrying our luggage down a sloping street. We disappeared through a large doorway and, still without spotting any external clues, realised we'd arrived at our hotel. We walked straight past a reception desk into a court yard area, a bright square dotted with plants and tables and chairs. Several smiling smartly dressed hotel staff greeted us with what looked like hedge leaves in cups of hot water. 'Welcome to Cusco. This is coca tea, the coca leaves will help you with the altitude.'

The coca plant flourishes in this area - these are the leaves that cocaine's derived from. It's a traditional stimulant, perfectly legal and not just available but an essential part of the diet of many local people. Visitors are encouraged to have the leaves as tea, especially if you're going up into the mountains. Locals tend to just chew them. With some uncertainty, everyone took a sip. It was definitely 'earthy' a little like drinking, well leaves from a hedge - I guess. Relieved to put the rucksack down I took a cup and sat down

- but after a few short minutes, we were on the move again to find our rooms.

There was a flurry of bags and bodies as a number of hotel staff darted around the courtyard and started carrying rucksacks to the rooms. In the bustle Rose and I found our room key, grabbed our smaller bags and were directed to the stairs to get to our room on the first floor. Rose was in front and I wondered why she stopped suddenly, six steps up. After I'd taken a couple I realised why. I was dizzy and struggling to get my breath, feeling like I'd just ran up to the top of a lighthouse. 'You have to go slowly,' Rose gasped. I just nodded in reply, taken by surprise that something as simple as going up a dozen stairs was taking so much effort. I gratefully passed my backpack to one of the hotel staff who smiled and leapt past as I struggled to put one foot in front of the other. Rose and I stopped for breath at the top and looked at each other. "Wow," we both exclaimed at the same time.

3 Sick and Tired

'Traveling is a brutality. It forces you to trust strangers and to lose sight of all that familiar comfort of home and friends.' Cesare Pavese

We'd been given instructions to have a quick change if we needed and be back down in the courtyard in half an hour. I knew if I was on my own I would definitely by now be heading for a lie down but, as I was in a group, I really had to try to do the group thing. Having a nap and then wandering around on my own was probably not going to be very 'group thing'. This was also the only day we had in Cusco and I didn't want to miss out on it. I hoped a shower and coffee would perk me up and keep me going for the rest of the afternoon.

As we walked into our room Rose and I both sniffed. "What is that smell?" It was definitely something aromatic and smokey. We debated if it was a 'herbal' type of cigarette - then realised it was incense. Burning incense seemed to be the equivalent of a giving a room a squirt of air freshener and it became a familiar smell when we went into buildings. The room was basic but clean and we each claimed one of the good sized beds and had a quick wash. It was good to at least get out of the clothes I'd travelled all that way in.

After regrouping in the courtyard we were told a bit more about the rest of the day. We'd head to the main square and onto a restaurant for lunch, go on a guided tour for the rest of the afternoon, then back to the hotel to get changed and have a briefing about the trek before heading out for dinner. I wondered if I could squeeze a sleep in at some point. I took some paracetamol to ward off a headache that had been simmering for a while and glugged a bottle of water. We had been told filtered water would be available for us all of the time and we must make sure we drank lots of it. We'd taken this to heart and already nearly emptied a large container on the table in the courtyard.

We walked back into the narrow street outside, which sloped steeply down then flattened and widened out onto a square. Tiny cars that looked like they'd been squashed up by a car crusher rumbled along the narrow stony roads. We were at Plaza de Armas, the large main square with a fountain at the centre, bordered by low Spanish colonial style buildings complete with shutters and balconies. At one side, the Cathedral of Santa Dominica dominates and is flanked by the Church de la Compañía de Jesus. These two buildings are the tallest around, their spires piercing the blue sky, but the backdrop to everything is the mountains, which made all else feel small and compact.

Like so much of Inca history there are a lot of unknowns about Cusco. There is no definitive answer to when or why it was built. It is thought to date from the 13th Century, and been built in the shape of a puma, a sacred animal to the Incas. The Spanish first arrived in the city in 1533 and went on to destroy many of the buildings. Despite resistance from the Incas and a ten month siege,

Cusco became the centre for the Spanish colonisation of the Andes and new buildings were built on top of old Inca walls. In 1950 an earthquake damaged many of these buildings but all of the Inca architecture was left intact.

Peru declared independence in 1821 and Cusco continued to grow as an important administrative and trading centre. Since the 1990s it has become a key tourist destination, and it has also in recent years experienced a burst in population growth, which is now over half a million people.

Despite the recent expansion, it felt uncrowded, with a relaxed air, people stood chatting or sitting on benches, nodding to acquaintances. As many people wore the brightly coloured traditional clothing as those in modern style like jeans and T-shirts. It gave me the impression of a place where the old and new can be content together, not entirely blending but rather rubbing along without any friction.

The cloudless sky reeked of heat and I could feel the sun's rays getting to work on my peaky pale skin within a couple of minutes. Paco, our other guide who was more cuddly bear to Tony's action man, offered to take a group photograph and took our cameras from us. In a scene that became a regular on the trip, Paco stood with cameras dangling like jewellery from both arms and his neck, looking like one very overenthusiastic tourist.

On Tony's advice the first thing was to change our money. Tony pointed out a money exchange he said was a 'trusted' one. It was an open fronted kiosk size shop, there were many similar shops around the square, slightly hidden and easy to miss at first. As I waited my turn to go in, with no room for more than four at a time inside, I felt like I was on a school trip.

Heading to the restaurant for lunch we passed a small lady wearing a tall hat nearly the size of her body, engrossed in conversation with another who was holding a rope. I took a second glance that confirmed on the end of the rope was a llama. Or alpaca. At this point we couldn't tell the difference, only that it was definitely not a dog she was walking.

The centre was very neatly laid out in a grid like way, streets stretched out from each corner of the plaza. We headed up a steep narrow one, flanked by large blocks of stones making up walls. Inca walls. No mortar or glue needed, just immense precision and individually built bricks interlocking, strong enough to withstand the earthquakes that destroyed other buildings.

I looked up as we headed up a steep lane and saw the others walking ahead. My head was thumping and I was starting to struggle to breathe. Small steps, don't rush I reminded myself as I got slower and slower. By the time I reached the top I had to stop to get my breath. We had arrived at a restaurant and walked through the bright blue doorway. We were shown seats at a long table in a courtyard, with a huge open clay oven in the middle. A kind of outdoor Cusco pizza parlour. I reckoned it was now about 48 hours since I'd eaten any proper food and couldn't wait to tuck in. Down one wall were buckets of potatoes, red, yellow, brown, who knew you could get so many different looking ones but you can in Peru - apparently 2,000 different varieties.

The air filled with the noise of conversation and after ordering a drink and vegetarian pizza I couldn't seem to keep up with any of them. I felt dizzy as I stood up to find the toilet. Jo came with me and when she asked if I was okay I admitted I wasn't feeling too good but it was probably just tiredness. As we came back and sat down my pizza arrived but my appetite had just vanished. I couldn't touch the freshly cooked pizza that ten minutes ago had been so appealing. Paco sitting near me noticed everyone but me tucking in. "Not good? Do you want something else? We can change it." I felt worse, not wanting to seem rude, not wanting to make a fuss and definitely not wanting to be the first one to be ill. I had a horrible rush of heat and for a mortifying moment thought I was going to throw up there and then. All I could think of was how utterly embarrassing that would be. "I'm just going to go back to the hotel and lie down I think," I muttered to Jo as I stood up. Before I could make my way out Tony was at my side. I just wanted to get back to the hotel as quickly as possible.

Despite my protests that I could find my way back Tony insisted on taking me there. In reality it was just as well as I wouldn't have found my way back. I didn't even know the name of the hotel let along which street it was in. I was conscious of chattering rapidly to Tony on the way, wanting to get back to the hotel faster than my legs could go. I had to get back as soon as I could but wanted to reassure him I was okay. I was relieved to reach the hotel and smiled as best I could at Tony's concerned face. No, he didn't need to stay. I'd be fine after a sleep. No, he really didn't need to see me to my room. I waved him away as we reached the reception. With impeccable timing I made it up the stairs, into the room, into the bathroom and threw up.

After vomiting until I couldn't any more and with my head thumping, I closed my eyes and sank into sleep. There's a great belief in my family that sleep is a cure for pretty much everything that doesn't need operating on and I had faith that I'd wake up feeling, if not 100 per cent, at least a lot better.

I came round as I heard the door opening and could sense Rose walking round carefully trying not to wake me. I slowly opened my eyes just a little. I muttered hello and briefly absorbed Rose's words that we had another hour or so until we had to get up and out for a briefing and dinner, and I fell back asleep.

I woke again and sat up at the same time as Rose who'd had a nap. "How are you feeling?" she asked. "Better," I said, taking a sip of water. I felt fairly light headed which I put down to the lack of food and a bit shivery - but the temperature had dropped quite rapidly. I had a wash and caught up on Rosie's news from their tour round Cusco. Still shivering, I put my jacket on and we went downstairs to the room where everyone had gathered with the

27

guides. There was chatter between small groups as friendships had started to form.

As Tony and Paco gave out sheets of paper I felt a wave of nausea rising. On the way down, I'd already spotted the nearest toilet so ran to it just in time. I rejoined the group but after another sharp exit said I was going back to the room. Tony and Paco came up to me, looking concerned. I struggled to hear exactly what they were saying but caught mention of 'The Doctor' and guessed they weren't referring to the Time Lord version. Insisting that I just needed to sleep, I agreed to Paco bringing the doctor to see me, and Rose came with me back to our room.

There was a knock and Rose opened the door. Paco came in and introduced the Doctor whose name I didn't remember. He was due to be with us for the duration of the trek. He may not have expected to be needed quite so soon.

The Doctor spoke very little English, so Paco turned interpreter - except I was struggling to understand him too. Rose joined in and, in between breaking off as I went to the bathroom, we managed between us to have a conversation. This went along the lines of :

"Take a tablet", as I was handed a large brown lozenge.

"I can't, I keep throwing up" - perfectly timed dash to the toilet so also giving practical example.

"You'll be dehydrated, I will check your oxygen level" - cue sticking vice like grip thing on end of finger.

"Yes, your oxygen is too low, you have altitude sickness.'

"I'll be fine if I just sleep" - cue some debate in Spanish.

"Do you have insurance?"

"Yes I took it out through Charity Challenge." - heads nodded.

"Doctor would like you to go to his hospital. It's not far, you can get oxygen and be rehydrated"

"Oh no, really, I'll be fine if I just get some sleep" - cue some muttering and shaking of heads.

Rose assured me she'd come with me, ignoring my protests she'd miss her night out, insisting she wasn't hungry. Reluctantly I agreed to go to the hospital and asked how long I'd be there for. I started resisting again when they said I'd have to really stay in overnight but was placated by the promise I'd be in my own room. Starting to feel too exhausted to protest any further, I grabbed a few bits and was reminded take insurance documents and passport. Rose was more on the ball and also grabbed a couple of plastic bags.

Outside the hotel we squashed into one of the tiny cars. Doctor chatting to the taxi driver in the front with Tony, Rose and I knee to knee in the back. I retched as quietly as I could into the plastic bags during the journey that seemed to take forever but in reality probably lasted ten minutes.

We arrived in a brightly lit building and after conversations in Spanish, I was shown into a room with a bed in it. A man wearing the recognisable global uniform of white coat introduced himself as Doctor Dante, and asked "You have insurance?" Once this life-threatening question was clarified, I changed into a hospital gown, climbed into the bed and was given an oxygen mask.

A seeming gaggle of white coats (in reality Dr Dante and a nurse or two) tried to stab something into my veins which are renowned for their disappearing act. Their kit, in what looked like the type of tool box you buy in B&Q was dropped on the floor and the instruments hastily put back in. The floor was also the repository for the wrappings the needles came in, bits of bloodied cotton wool and anything else that needed 'binned'.

A person not in a white coat came into the room with the insurance documents that Rose had handed to them. "This number isn't working - have you a certificate?" After much debate, frowns (on their part), confusion (on mine and Rose's) she went away seemingly doubtful that I actually had insurance. When she came back in she handed me a phone. On the other end a voice started asking questions that I couldn't understand let alone answer, so Rose took the phone and scribbled things down. It turned out that the phone number on the policy document (which was the only thing I had taken) was wrong. I was told I had to have an agreement from the insurance company for them to go ahead with any treatment. After a tricky conversation with the wrong person on the phone Rose finally got a different number. She rang and got an agreement that someone would fax a note to confirm that the insurance would cover my treatment. But - given it was now very late on a Saturday night they might not do this until the morning.

This seemed to be placate everyone and, after hooking me up to a drip, the white coats disappeared out of the door. Tony appeared at the bedside with his permanent slightly worried expression. "We'll go now, someone will come for you in the morning though. OK?" I nodded as they left and closed my eyes again. Being left in a strange city in hospital all by myself was not been quite the first night I had imagined, but I was too exhausted to care.

4 Back on Track

'Not all those who wander are lost' - J R R Tolkein

'Well guess who was the first to fall victim to that altitude (tho I also blame lack of sleep & those flights!) & spend her first night in cusco in a hospital?? And we're not even up that mountain yet.
Still haven't let me out, oxygen too low & heart rate too high, no one else here so dealing with limited English speaking medical people, now told insurance company isn't responding & I'll have to pay cash!! Plus cleaner cleaning the toilet and NOT WEARING GLOVES!! X'

'NIGHTMARE! WHICH INSURANCE? CAN U CONTACT THE TRAVEL CO? HAV U ENUFF MONEY?'

'Insurance co booked thru charity challenge co! I brought only policy doc not cert (oops) there was wrong number on that, finally spoke to them last night but clinic had no response this morning. No idea re cost. I have 400 dollars cash & about same on credit card. Can't let anyone at home know - imagine the panic. And no friends here!!! No food or drink either!'

'Just been presented with bill. 472.69 dollars. Most expensive night I've ever had'

'NO. CANT TELL FAMILY. DID CHARITY TAKE U TO HOSP? HOW MANY HOURS AGO? CAN U FONE LOCAL REP? DONT WORRY ABOUT MONEY. CAN ALWAYS SEND.IS THERE A WESTERN UNION IN CUSCO?'

'See if I can pay half cash half credit card. Rep brought me here last night but has taken rest of group out for the day! Going to get dressed and get back to hotel - arggh dont even know where i am or whats its called!! X'

'FOUND 9 WES UN PLACES. IT WILL HELP IF U HAV AN ADDRESS! ARE U OK NOW OR HAVE THEY BOOTED U OUT AS A TROUBLE MAKER? X'

'Just about to negotiate with the terrier with the bill!! X'

'TAKE YOUR TIME. A BRAIN STARVED OF OXYGEN IS NOT RATIONAL! GET HOTEL DETAILS. DO NOT GO ON HUNT FOR CHOC MUSEUM. X'

'Now back at hotel. A rep came to meet me not one from yesterday. He followed me out & doesn't speak English so I thought he was trying to accost me! Going to shower, go for wander & get something to eat. Must get sense of humour & adventure back before the girly group returns! X

I'd woken the next morning to an early visit from Dr Dante whose first words were not 'how are you feeling' but 'we have not heard from the insurance company.' After doing his stethoscope and clip on end of finger tests, he declared that I couldn't yet go and left the room. Apparently my oxygen level was too low and heart rate too high - even after being fed oxygen through tubes attached with pincers to my nostrils and hooked up to an intravenous saline drip all night. Still attached to the drip, I looked round and realised to my relief there was an en suite - or at least a toilet with the door near to my bed. I unclipped the oxygen tube and wheeled the pole with me so I could go to the loo.

As I climbed back into the bed, feeling slightly wobbly, a smiling white coated lady came in holding a tray with a slice of toast and cup of tea on it. I said 'gracias' as she hurried out again and drank the tea, wondering when someone would come to get me out. I could see shadows across the frosted window occasionally walking past the room but no one else came in. I texted Rose, telling her I was ok but they weren't letting me leave yet and asking if she knew whether Tony was coming for me. She said he was preparing to take the rest of the group out for the day. She spoke to him, and he said someone from the company would be there later in the morning to collect me.

A small, fierce looking lady came in the room, papers in hand, telling me that I'd have to pay before I left because the insurance company weren't responding. After a brief exchange which didn't really resolve anything apart from realisation that neither of us could speak the others language, she left. I was alone with too much time and too little oxygen. What if I didn't have enough money? What would they do? What if I wasn't well enough to go on the trek? What would happen? Where was I? How would I get back to the hotel? Why did I want to do this? Bored, lonely and close to tears, I started texting a friend back in England. Although worried that my phone battery was running down, I was glad of some reassuring contact from back home, however distant.

Eventually Dr Dante returned flanked by another non English speaking nurse and the fierce paper waving woman. I persuaded him that I was okay to leave, despite his misgivings, and negotiated with the fierce one to pay half cash and half on credit card. The only thing I wanted to do was get out of there. The fact that I didn't know where the hospital was or actually even the name of the hotel I had to get back to wasn't an issue. At least not until I paid and then stood with my bag in the entrance way, wondering what to do next. The lady at reception had turned her back on me to deal with people who had just come in. I was obviously dismissed.

Walking into the glare of the sunshine, I realised I was lost but was glad to stand at the top of the steps outside and breathe the air, despite it not obviously not having enough oxygen for my requirements. As I stood there, I was aware that a man who'd been hanging around the reception area had followed me out. He came up to me saying something about a taxi. "No thanks. I don't speak Spanish," I said turning my back on him. But he was persistent, chattering on in Spanish, despite me moving away, mentioning 'taxi' and pointing to his jacket. It took a few minutes before I realised he was pointing to the logo that had the name of our tour company on it. He was the rep who'd come to collect me. Too relieved to feel foolish, I smiled and nodded, "taxi back to the hotel?" "Si" he said, also looking relieved.

He flagged down a squished car and we drove in silence back to the one street familiar to me that the hotel was in. I thanked him as he got out and he came with me through the doors and to reception. "I'm ok now thanks," I said, having decided I'd shower, get changed and go out. He gestured, pointing to the ground, "You... here." "No thanks I am going to go out," I said, also pointing and doing the very English thing of raising my voice. "No, no, here," he looked concerned but I had no intention of wasting more time sitting in a room by myself. "No I am going out. Into Cusco," I pointed to the door. He turned and spoke in Spanish to the man on reception. He took a printed map and marked a cross where the hotel was and handed it to me. We were at Hotel Garcilaso - if I couldn't remember it I now had it written down. That would do me. I smiled and thanked him as I headed for my room.

I still felt light headed and wobbly but put that down to lack of food. It was after 1pm, I'd had a text from Rosie and I'd told her I was going to go out and find a cafe. She reckoned the group would be back in about an hour so I wouldn't be on my own too long. After a tepid shower and change of clothes I headed out, walking slowly as the heat and altitude hit me. I realised I probably didn't want to wander too far - as my friend had pointed out in her text, an oxygen starved brain does not make for quick thinking. I meandered into a cafe in a side street and ordered a large coffee, pleased I managed to do so in a kind of Spanish. My head started to hurt a little and I felt a bit nauseous so only took a couple of sips, but was content to just sit in the empty cafe listening to the waitress chat indecipherably on to her friend. I got a text from Rose and arranged to meet her and the others as they'd got back from their day. I made my way carefully back to the main square.

As the group arrived, I felt slightly overwhelmed with the questions, chatter and general melee so was glad when Rose took my arm and suggested getting something to eat. We found another cafe and navigated our way through the menu, this time I avoided coffee, getting water and a sandwich. I left the filling but ate the bread - which was sweet, a little like brioche and delicious. Rose told me that that's what the bread was like that they'd had and chattered on about the day I'd missed out on. They'd gone to an Inca site just outside of the city and walked for a few hours. She said it wasn't just the ruins and landscape that was amazing - they'd also met the rest of our support crew there. In the team who'd be with us on the trek was a chef and assistants, complete with a tent for cooking in and one for dining in. Chef and his able assistants had thrown together an amazing three course meal including a dessert apparently to die for. As I listened to Rose describe their day, I knew that whatever Doctor or anyone might say I definitely still wanted to do the trek - I'd come too far not to.

We had a schedule to stick to, so went back to the hotel to change in time for a briefing down stairs before going out to dinner. Gathering in the room for the briefing, the guides welcomed me back, Tony with a worried smile, while Paco gave me a broad grin and a kiss. I was pleased nobody was talking about me not being able to go on the trek, I said I was feeling fine and that seemed reassuring enough. Although I'd been reluctant to take tablets I was given Diamox to help deal with the altitude. In our pre-departure emails it was one of the things we'd discussed. Some of the group had taken them anyway as a precaution, others had brought them with them, though one girl's doctor back in England had refused to give her them. Side effects were limited but slightly odd including pins and needles in fingers and toes and the ability to make fizzy drinks taste flat.

It seemed that nobody had taken in much of the briefing the previous night. We blamed the altitude, having already had its wicked way with me it soon became the whipping boy for everything, related or not. Tony, with his semi concerned, fatherly expression, patiently went through the itinerary again.

We were trekking the Lares Valley trail. Tony explained that when he had started out, a good few years ago, before his hair turned silver, the ubiquitous Inca Trail to Machu Picchu was still relatively undiscovered. Only a few hardy or hippy souls wanted to go along the ancient route. Now, given the popularity, it was a bit 'spoilt' and very busy, full of tourists. The Lares Valley route Tony said, was his favourite - still unspoilt, relatively unknown and used by few people. He told us we'd be unlikely to meet anyone other than the families who live in the mountains. Our departure the next morning would start early with a four hour journey in the coach 'up, up, up' taking us into the Andes. We would be dropped off at Lares hot springs, natural pools with alleged health benefits for a dip and lunch. Then the trek would start properly. In the afternoon we'd also stop off at a school and spend time in a classroom. We were camping out in the mountains for the first two nights - while the trekking was very much ascending during most of the day, we'd head downwards to campsites at lower altitude. Apparently lack of oxygen can be bad for you whether awake or asleep. As well as Tony. Paco, and Doctor, there was chef and a small crew who would be with us throughout the mountain trek. At each camp site local men were hired to help set up and clear away after us.

Tony was aware that our attention span was short and as the sound of chatter started up and most questions were around toilets (none during the day when were walking, only at campsites) and showers (none until we get to a hotel), he drew the session to a close. "We will brief you every morning and as we go along. It is a lot to take in sometimes." The one point he was keen to get us to remember was to be on time. We had a schedule, we needed to stick to it and had to get to certain places at particular times. In answer to another question he said, no he had never led an all female group before. It was going to be a whole new experience for him too.

As the noise grew, he and Paco led us out of the hotel and towards the plaza. It was illuminated by the church and street lights and those coming from the kiosks and shops around the square. There were people sitting on the balconies above in restaurants and cafes and cars were still hurrying past. Along a narrow street we entered a restaurant called Incanto, which inside was bright and modern looking. We were led towards the back, where the kitchen was open for all to see, and sat at a long table that had been reserved.

Glancing at the menu reminded me I hadn't eaten properly for ages. The menu seemed to have elements of Spanish, Italian and Asian cuisine. There were a choice of vegetarian options which was a pleasant surprise. The rest of the group had been to quite a different style of restaurant the previous night, more traditional with pan pipers and a bar man who showed them how to mix Pisco sours. This is the local drink and as we were welcomed with a free one here it seemed rude not to at least try it. Pisco is a liquer, a grape brandy which when mixed with lime juice and egg white becomes a very quaffable if rather potent cocktail. A white, frothy short drink, it went down very well. But given the altitude and the very early start in the morning, after one everyone went onto soft drinks.

I opted for a beautifully presented bruschetta for starters, and a more traditional vegetable and quinoa main dish. Grains are staple crops here and quinoa is one of the most widely used ones, scattered in soups, stir fries, stews. The dessert that Rose had mentioned that chef had served them at lunch time was on the menu. The Peruvians seem to have a real sweet tooth and the Tres Leche is literally, three milk pudding. It's basically a cake soaked in condensed milk, evaporated milk AND cream - with a bit of Peruvian fruit like lucuma thrown in as a healthy after thought. Strangely not too sweet or sickly, it's calorific value and fat content was best not thought about. And I did need to build myself up for the trek, of course...

The meals were all included so not having to pay and go through the usual complexities of working out who had what was odd at first but very welcome given the size of the group. All we needed to pay for were any drinks and contribution for a tip. This was easily sorted and we wandered our way back to the hotel through the cobbled streets. Everywhere led back to the main plaza which was already a familiar landmark. From there it was easy to find our way.

The part of Tony's briefing we had absorbed was that we had to be up, packed, had breakfast and ready to leave by 6.30am the next morning. Rose and I decided we needed to pack before going bed rather than leave it until the morning. Back in our room we struggled to work out what we needed to pack into which bags. We had been given an extra bag which would be taken on the trek and given to us at the campsites. Then we also had our large rucksacks which we were leaving behind at this hotel which we'd be coming back to at the end of the trip. Then there was another bag that would appear at the hotel near Machu Picchu we'd be staying in towards the end of the trek. And not forgetting our day packs that would hold all of the gear we'd need while walking during the day. Confusing enough, made more confusing by being tired and having a fuzzy head. We did our best before we both fell gratefully into bed for much needed sleep. We'd find out as the week went on what bits we'd packed in the wrong bags. We would of course be able to blame the altitude.

5 Long and winding road

'Crashes are common on the treacherous winding mountain roads of the Peruvian highlands. According to the Associated Press, more than 4,000 people died in such accidents last year.'
Los Angeles Times

I felt like I'd been asleep only for minutes when the alarms went off. Rose and I groaned greetings at each other before agreeing the bathroom rota. We opted not to check what we'd packed into our bags the night before and just trust that we'd have everything we need.

Breakfast was hurried, with little time to enjoy the varied spread of bread, fruit, cereals, cheese and meat. Although we were encouraged of course to have the coca tea, the coffee tasted decidedly better. After a short spell of chaos, as we had to leave the different bags in different places, we somehow managed to be get onto the coach and ready for off just about on time.

Once out of the centre of the city, the road started climbing immediately. As we rose higher, looking down on the red tiled roofs, I could see that Cusco sprawled out further than I thought at the bottom of the valley. We were heading up the mountains that served as such a dramatic backdrop to the streets and buildings in the city below. We reached a slight plateau and came close up to a huge statue of Jesus, arms outstretched, like a much smaller version of Rio's Christ the Redeemer. The white stone figure is lit up at night, and as we'd noticed the evening before, could be seen from all over the city. Known as Christo Blanco, it was built by a group of Christian Palestinians that were given refuge in Cusco in 1945. A symbol of gratitude, it was a parting gift before they finally returned to their home country. It's said the statue is a reminder to the people of Cusco that good deeds don't go unnoticed.

The narrow road we were on twisted and turned, climbing ever upward, the drop on one side getting longer as we climbed. Llamas and alpacas loped around the sides of the mountain like overgrown sheep, heads down pulling at scattered tufts of grass. The bus suddenly slowed and juddered to a halt. There were two small colourfully clad people with several horses approaching in front of the bus. Our vehicle took up the whole width of the road. On the left hand side was a wall of rocks, on the other side was a sheer drop. There was a momentary stand off. The bus definitely wasn't moving and they didn't seem too keen to either.

The horses took the initiative and started to edge round the bus on the side with the drop, hooves making stones and earth tumble down to the ground many metres below. The Peruvians followed their horses and inside the bus was a collective sigh of relief as horses and people made it past. Once they were safely behind us we went forward again.

The journey carried on like the longest, scariest fairground ride in the world. Those sitting near the front got a view that looked like we were heading over the edge every time there was a sharp corner, which was about every 500 metres. Because we were zig zagging as well as going upwards, whichever side you were on you took a turn in thinking the bus was hanging over the edge. Looking out of a window on the side I was, I couldn't see any road, or track as it was now, at all between us and the ever increasing drop down the side of the mountain.

I could feel the altitude affecting me again and my head was thumping when the bus pulled to a stop. We were next to a sign, a rare thing, that told us we were at 4,600 metres. It was time for a break, a photo opportunity and the chance to add our own little pile of rocks to the cairns people left up here for good luck. It was also a chance for our first communal outdoor toilet experience. We created our own river by having a mass squat behind the bus - an instant bonding moment. As we got back on the bus with a loud outburst of hysterical giggling, we put it down to 'altitude'.

We made steady progress crawling round hairpin bends and manoeuvring around boulders that had fallen down into the road. We didn't see any other vehicles - until we were brought to a halt by a massive crane blocking the road. It was heading the same way as us and, although it had managed somehow to get that far, it was having problems negotiating the next bend. The only way was up. There was no way back, no room to turn around, no way to reverse down. We sat stationary for 15 minutes as two men, one driving the other standing outside directing him, shouted and gesticulated at each other. The huge crane finally inched around the corner, constantly threatening to tumble over the edge. I closed my eyes as our driver then squeezed our bus past the machine, not wanting to stay crawling behind it. A little further on there was a massive boulder in the middle of the road, which we had problems getting around. I wondered what on earth would happen to the crane, it looked like it would be impossible for it to get any further. If you are ever on a road going up a mountain near Cusco, beware the abandoned crane.

Breaking up our four hour journey, we were stopping at Lares market. I envisaged quite a large town, a load of market stalls, tourists browsing among them, my first chance to buy and haggle. We got to Lares, passing its sign and arriving at the market place in the same breath. The only other vehicles were a couple of scooters and a police car, so the bus just parked where it stopped in the small square. The people were all dressed in the traditional clothing, standing and sitting in small groups, and gave disinterested glances as we climbed off. This was a proper market for locals not for bus loads of tourists. The stalls were piled with varied fruit and veg and brightly coloured bundles of wool. There wasn't much else, just what these people needed to live off and trade with each other. It felt like we were interrupting a close knit community get together where people came to socialise, eat and drink. Even the local police officers were standing chatting, hats off, drinking a beer. Community policing at its best.

We were neither welcomed nor put off, were merely tolerated as we weaved our way around the stalls, surreptitiously taking photographs. As we were getting back onto the bus I commented on a load of women piling up on the back of a Toyota truck, looking like a pyramid of colourful sacks. "It looks like they're trying for the world record of how many people can you get into a truck." Paco explained "The selling part of the market is finishing. That is the only truck that will take the women home. They have to go now and work in the house. The men stay and drink." Some things are the same the world over.

After Lares market, the next stop was to be the hot springs, where we'd say goodbye to the bus and start our trek from. With few clues that we were nearing it, the driver pulled up in front of a gateway. You would only get here with if you'd planned to - it wasn't a place you could bump into by accident. We'd had to turn off the 'main' road and come down a track which ended at the entrance. We got off and the bus turned round and headed off.

Tony led us through a gateway. Through the other side were a number of small pools that looked like they could be part of the rocky landscape. A couple of stone buildings were the only signs that anything here was purpose built. It was a remote but spectacular setting, nestling in a valley, mountains rising up either side.

We wandered past the gloopy looking, curry sauce coloured pools. The hot springs 'said to be very good for you, with special powers' sounded more inviting than they looked. Most of the girls had come prepared with a swimming costume and decided to give it a go. It hadn't been on my want to do list, even less so after already being ill, so I was sitting it out. A couple of others opted out as well and we sat on a grassy bank, enjoying the sunshine and entertained by the scenes in the pools. There were a couple of older men who we decided must be regulars, seeming to have a set sequence of ones they dipped in and out of, not staying more than a few minutes in each. The appearance of our gang from the changing room was accompanied by squeals as one by one they dipped toes in, then plunged fully into a pool. Tony gamely went in with them, looking a bit bashful to find himself surrounded by a giggling group of girls. Meanwhile Paco stayed out, sitting fully dressed by the side enjoying the view through his sunglasses.

While the girls moved around trying out different pools, our trek team put up the tent that was our canvas cafe. Next to it was the cooking tent, two sights that would become welcome and familiar landmarks on our trek. Water, handwash and towels were at the entrance and inside was a huge long table and seat, with cutlery, cups and condiments set out.

Dried and dressed again in the uniform of trek trousers and hiking boots, everyone trooped inside, the babble of noise rose and I caught pieces of conversation flying around. The springs had been hot but okay once you were in them; yes we'd get lunch and dinner cooked and set out in the tents for all meals on the trek; we must all eat and keep energy levels up; yes there were vegetarian options and a gluten free one.

Laughter started rising as the mustard bottle was passed around, it grew louder as more of the group got to see what it was called. It was Fanny Mustard - a brand name made, I am sure, much more amusing due to the altitude. The guides looked a bit bemused at the hoots as the bottle was passed up the table so those who were straining to see what the joke was could find out. "It's a funny word?" puzzled Paco. An entertaining five minutes took place trying to politely explain what this slang word was with lots of gesticulations. "Ohhhhhhh" he said, as he realised, and with a half embarrassed grin went on to explain in Spanish to the crew sitting near him, who burst out laughing.

The conversation continued discussing slang words. A Peruvian word for drink, Paco explained, was 'chichi' - but this sounded very close to the slang for... He made round orb movements from his chest, and we all cracked up laughing as someone was taking a photo. After this, 'say chichis' became a catchphrase for the rest of the trek, any time a camera pointed our way. And it works just as well as saying cheese.

Tony, with his fatherly concern, encouraged us all to tuck into the three course lunch. Taking his instructions that we must eat to keep energy going to heart, we filled up on cheese and bread, potato cakes for the veggies among us and fruit for afters, accompanied by juice and coca tea. A final trip to the toilet, which though basic would be luxury compared to what we'd have for the next couple of days, gave rise to more hysteria thanks to a lurking large spider. Screams and laughter led to pondering about how we'd manage in tents in the middle of mountains, with whatever might be out there.

As we sorted out our discarded rucksacks, we debated whether it was going to rain or not, what to wear - full waterproofs including trousers, fleece jackets, would it get cold? Tony never lost his smile but his expression grew slightly more anxious as he tried to tell us that really we were already a bit behind schedule and needed to get a move on. He was learning quickly that getting a large group of females to be ready on time was akin to herding cats. Noisy cats at that.

Then finally, at last, with no going back - we were off. This was going to be a bit of a test for me, the first time I had really walked any distance in this very foreign environment that had already taken me by surprise. I decided to stay at the back, my usual pace and impatience was going to have to take a back seat. We set off through the gateway and back up the hill. We'd come down it in the bus of course and not realised just how steep it was.

At the side of the path was a long ditch that was being dug and cleared by a line of local people. Most didn't even look up as we approached but one lady had stopped and was talking to Paco. The state, he explained, requires that every family has to give a certain amount of time to doing something in the community. These people were keeping the drains clear. Her husband was away working so she had to be the one to come and do the work- it's compulsory. "Do you see that bundle on her back?" he asked. I nodded. The woman had a bright woven cloth hanging like a sack on her back, bulging at the bottom with its contents. "She has her child in there. She has no one at home to look after her." She returned to the quiet, industrious line.

With the sun beating down and the steepness of the hill, it was easy to justify having to walk quite so slowly. Coming to a relatively flat stretch, the need to walk much slower than normal, actually having to concentrate on breathing, stopping regularly for a break was a reminder of the height we were already at. I judged how well I was coping by whether I could walk and talk or not - until I realised that actually talking wasn't helping at all. The group had split naturally into two or three groups. I was happy to hang back, bringing up the rear with Rose, Andrea, Suzanne and Faye. I was in no hurry, even if I could have gone faster I didn't want to. I wanted to look around, take in as much as I could, conscious that I'd likely never be here doing this ever again.

6 Learning Lessons

'Children must walk several hours to the nearest elementary school and high schools are often only located in larger towns, too far from home for students to commute daily. While boys often move to urban centers to pursue an education, this same opportunity is not available for many girls. Only 3 in every 10 Peruvian girls from rural Andean communities enrol into high school.' Sacred Valley Project

We walked steadily onwards, always upwards. Tony, with our group at the back, was happy to point out things and answer my questions about strange looking flora and fauna. Having been born and lived all his life in Peru his love of the country was obvious and his knowledge was impressive. He'd travelled all over and also worked as a guide in other parts of South America. As it's mainly seasonal work he had his fingers in many other pies as well, including crafting silver jewellery. Always active, as you could tell by his wiry frame, he told me he loved trekking, mountain climbing and kayaking in particular.

The valley below with the river snaking through it was getting more distant. The colours became more muted, and trees and bushes more sparse. There were no fields of crops, just the occasional allotment type square of sprouting vegetables close to a stone building. We were now well away from the ease of modern life. Here to survive, people have to be self sufficient.

It's a lifestyle that's changed little over hundreds of years. Living off their own plot of land people grow vegetables and tend their own few animals. Alpacas are vital for both meat and wool. What's not needed by the family will be sold or swapped, at markets like the one we stopped at. We were walking on what was the main road - a dusty track. We didn't see any vehicles, no cars, no tractors, not even a motor bike or cycle. If you've got a pair of legs you've got your own transport. As we walked slowly, breathing heavily, three tiny ladies came scurrying past, humps of coloured bundles on their backs, which could have had vegetables or small children in them. We were twice as tall and twice as slow.

We were due to call into a school along the way, to meet a class and talk to the teacher. Tony checked his watch and smiled his worried smile as we approached a long wall at the side of the road. 'I think we will be too late. School finishes at 1pm', he said stopping next to a gateway. Inside, next to a long single storey building we spotted the rest of the group who had got there before us, with some children coming out to greet them. It had been suggested we bring notebooks, paper, pens and pencils and everyone had something. Jo had brought some balloons and was showing an eager, red cheeked little girl how to blow it up. She was giving all she got and gave a broad grin when she succeeded.

School had finished for the day but the teacher and several of the children were still there, waiting to meet us. The building had murals of cartoon characters on the outside, inside we crowded into a small classroom. It was furnished with the type of mini chairs and desks familiar to anyone with children at primary school. The cut out paper shapes and paintings on the walls and chalk drawings on the blackboard were familiar signs of a school anywhere. But then I noticed there were no computers, the furniture was old style wooden single desks and chairs, there was a lack of books, shelves, games, boxes of brightly coloured stuff you usually find in primary schools.

Half a dozen pairs of deep brown eyes looked at us, curious but shy. One boy and one girl stood at the front with a teacher, their clothes an eclectic mix of traditional and modern - bright colours, little round hats, school jumpers, jogging pants, trainers. "We are the only school in the area, the children walk here for a start at 8am. We teach Spanish and English but many of the families and older people only speak Quechuan," the teacher explained, introducing the children. A drawing of a cat looks the same in any language and as she drew the familiar two circles for head and body and lines for whiskers the children wrote on the board in Spanish then one of our group was invited to write in English.

Also familiar was the song they started performing for us. When they started singing it in English we all joined in with a rousing burst of Hands, Shoulders, Knees and Toes. As we left, feeling both cheered and also reflective on how very different the lives of these children are, one girl set off determinedly in front of us, disappearing up the dusty path. "Where on earth does she live?" I asked Tony. "They come from miles and miles around. The children sometimes walk well over an hour or two to get to school and then the same back home," he said. I mused how my son moans about getting a 20 minute bus ride.

We were now walking again split into our two or three groups and at the back we quite often lost sight of the others, just going our own pace. Our route was a consistent upward one, occasionally my head would thump and my breathing would worsen. I guessed that that was when, even if it wasn't obvious, we were suddenly climbing more steeply. By now everyone had stripped off the waterproofs and layers as the sun was beating down, intense and quite uncomfortable. As we carried on there was a camaraderie growing in the little group I was with. Everyone was occasionally struggling at times in the heat and it was difficult sometimes to speak. Stopping for breath was a chance to check everyone was alright, quench thirst and also drink in the view which was changing. The scenery was getting sparser, stone houses a more rare sight, the foliage was dropping away to reveal a more barren, brown landscape.

After some time, I felt like I was starting to struggle. Although we probably hadn't walked far in terms of distance, we had been going for several hours. It was all uphill and the sheer effort in doing normal things like walking and breathing was exhausting me. I turned round, hearing a stamping noise coming from behind.

Llamas, running like a herd of sheep, came loping along past us. Not the most elegant or natural runners, they looked like they would just mow down anything in their way. I wondered what had startled them, then spotted that following them were dots of red which became obvious as people as they got closer. It looked like a family, led by a couple of ladies - mother and daughter or two sisters? There were a handful of small children scattered around, running along, throwing curious looks our way as we took photos. One little boy in particular turned showman and jumped on top of rocks, arms out, smiling widely at us. Another little girl stopped to have her photo taken, staring at the camera boldly, unsmiling, serious. After much waving from us eventually a shy smile appeared across her face.

The herd and family were soon ahead of us, disappearing into the distance. They were, explained Paco, a family of farmers taking their llamas and couple of sheep down from the hills and home for the night. Something they'd do every day. But where did they live - I couldn't see any houses? He waved his arm, pointing in the distance 'a long way.' And why were there only women, where were the men? "Working somewhere else, probably. Or sometimes just at home."

Jo was walking with me, chatting on cheerily despite me feeling unable to respond. I was really starting to flag and was glad the track had flattened out. I didn't have a watch with me to check but it felt it was getting cold, like the sun was disappearing. All of sudden, having gone slightly ahead, Jo shouted, "Tents! I can see tents!" She waved at our rag tag bunch at the back and we peered to where she was pointing. I could just make out green shapes, a plume of smoke and figures milling about. We were nearly there. Home - for the night. Never did I think I'd be so glad to see a campsite.

The realisation that the end was indeed in sight, at least for the day, gave me a final burst of energy. The air was now decidedly chilly and damp. Clouds had suddenly come down, literally, and when we reached it the campsite was in the middle of them, looking like it was wrapped in a blanket of fog.

We were the last to arrive and I was pleased to see my tent buddy Claire there. Rose had problems with her back so had had to opt to have a fold up camp bed brought for her to sleep in. The size of this meant she'd be in her own tent. We'd given her some stick about the poor crew member having to carry an extra load, but it meant she'd hopefully get a painless night's sleep. Claire had signed up late in the day, on her own, and she and I had decided to share a tent. I was wary about sharing with someone I really didn't know but she was friendly and easy going, and I was so tired I cared a lot less than I thought I would. She waved a welcome, standing outside a tent smiling, "I bagged us this one, it's on the end so it should be easier to remember which one we're in." I looked at the line of identical green canvas triangles - she was right. I was glad she had worked this out, and decided we'd definitely get on. My brain was feeling woolly and useless. I was sure that not only would I easily forget which tent I was in, I wouldn't have realised this until I tried to find my way back to it. Probably in the middle of the night.

If I could have just lain down in the tent and gone to sleep there and then I would have done. But there was much to do, and an itinerary to stick to. The crew brought bowls of water to each tent so we could 'wash', or at least dip our feet. I wanted the loo and had spotted the toilet tents a fair distance away. I really wanted a cuppa even if it was coca tea. I also wanted to see what the local ladies, who had magically appeared and were patiently sitting on blankets with their goods, had to sell. But very first of all I had to find my bag and find out if I had packed the right things in the right one.

Claire was admirably organised. "I think we should only unpack what we need tonight and make sure we have out what we need for the morning. We can then be ready to just pack away our night things and be off quickly in the morning.'

Oh, the morning. I didn't even want to think about it. We'd already been warned there would be little time, it was an early start, we had to be up sharp, have a quick breakfast and set off. The identical black bags we'd packed back at the hotel had miraculously appeared and were piled up in front of the tents. I felt a minor panic as I looked at the tags and couldn't see mine. I looked again then called Claire over. No, we couldn't find mine. What would I do if it wasn't here? I could borrow something for night wear and just stick with the same clothes for tomorrow even if I'd be a bit smelly. Claire read my mind - "you can borrow my things" she reassured me. Paco came over, seeing us hunting around. "My bag's not here." I tried to sound calm. I knew I'd manage but, having already been centre of attention for all the wrong reasons, I didn't fancy doing it again. I was close to tears when Paco said, 'here it is' and held up my bag. "You couldn't find it?" he asked puzzled. Claire and I exchanged a glance and said simultaneously "Altitude!"

There was now no time to do anything other than sort out the unpacking and repacking of bags, have a quick 'wash' with a wet wipe, and change into suitable layers which built up from a base of thermal leggings and vest. Although the afternoon had been hot we had been warned that during the night the temperature dropped and it would get very cold.

I ventured outside, it was getting dark quickly and I wanted to check out the toilets while there was still some light to see the way. There had been some debate over exactly what was a 'long drop' toilet. The tiny canvas cubicles held a precarious portable seat for squatting on over a hole that the most unfortunate member of the team had to dig out to set up. But much worse, they then had to fill it in again after it had been filled in by us, when we left camp. There was a small bucket of something that looked like grey ash that we were supposed to shovel on each time we went - it soon ran out. The toilet paper was starting to shrivel with the damp and the cubicles were already getting a tangible smell to them. Added to this we had to climb over a ridge of potentially toe damaging rocks to get there, so Clare and I agreed that middle of the night toilet needs would be better done just round the back of the tent.

It was now dark enough to need a torch but the ladies were still sitting on their blankets outside as I passed them, the last one to go into the dining tent, its long table set for our candle lit dinner. One of the girls had not turned up, deciding she was too tired and had just wanted to stay in her tent to sleep. I felt quite envious but Tony was concerned. "Everyone must eat, you need the energy, you must all eat." There was a slightly tired atmosphere in the tent although there was still non-stop chatter. We sat wrapped up in our jackets and hats, head torches on, looking like the oddest dinner party guests ever. Although I thought I wasn't really hungry the three courses, starting with bread and cheese, a very tasty potato-cheese- quinoa main dish and dessert of fruit, went down surprisingly well.

Beforehand, when I'd tried to imagine what the trek would be like, I'd wondered what we'd do in the evenings after dinner, as it got dark so early and turned so very cold at night. As I almost crawled back to the tent as soon as I'd finished my dinner, and gratefully lay down, huddled in my sleeping bag, I had the answer - sleep. It was after all nearly 8pm.

7 The Peru Crew

'The indigenous Indians of Peru are unique in the modern world. They are uniformly spiritual, uninterested in politics, and loyal to their families; they are not greedy or materialistic; they express themselves in shy smiles and rarely complain. Their pride is intact despite the almost inhumane solitude of the Altiplano and dismal treatment by the last 500 years of history.' Quechua Benefit

I woke to a distant rustling and muffled voices. Claire wriggled in her sleeping bag and croaked 'morning'. We sat up wrapped like caterpillars in our bedding, exchanging surprise at how well we'd slept. I'd stripped down to my thermal vest and had kept warm enough, though the damp was another issue. Everything smelled of wetness and mould in the making. A voice called gently "Hello. Tea." I unzipped our tent to find two of the crew with steaming kettle, cups and bowl. Without a watch I wasn't sure what time it was but it was early enough to not yet be light. The crew were bringing round coca tea and filling bowls for us to wash in - luxury room service for cold, damp trekkers.

As I stretched outside the tent I realised the noise and shadows I'd seen last night belonged to a group of ponies who were now grazing nearby. They glanced up quite disinterested as I had to take my first unavoidable trip to the so 'long drop' toilets, which were by now so full that there was very little 'drop' to be had.

The local ladies were already sitting as if they'd been on an all night vigil outside the dining tent. As we headed towards them for breakfast their bright colours stood out against the morning's dull mist. I had a quick glance at their selection of goods - hand woven socks, purses, bags, pieces of cloth, and half a dozen random bottles of water and that old favourite Inca Kola. I smiled and they stared back - not hostile or rude, it just seemed as if they didn't see the point of putting on a false or polite smile. Or maybe they had actually sat there all night, in which case not smiling was totally understandable.

"How much?" I asked holding up a pair of rather long, hairy socks, possibly llama or alpaca. I wasn't sure how to tell the difference and thought asking questions would likely be difficult and involve lots of sign language. One serious looking lady held up seven fingers. I did a quick calculation based on my own easy to remember though probably inaccurate way to convert money. We'd had a debate in the group about the local currency, the Nuevo Sol, and the exchange rate. I like an easy to use calculation so I'd plumped for 10 Sols equating to about £2.50. I didn't know how much seven was but it was less than £2.50 obviously. We exchanged and she nodded as she took the money. I thought perhaps that was the equivalent of a smile.

Toilets were becoming a regular topic of conversation even over breakfast. We compared notes on whether it had been worth the potentially toe stubbing treacherous trip in the middle of the night or just much better to do a round the back of the tent squat. It's fascinating how acceptable what would be considered unacceptable behaviour at home becomes when away.

Tony looked relieved that we'd had all made it safely through the night and with his paternalistic concern was reminding us all to eat up, we'd need lots of energy. Today, he told us, we had a hard walk ahead - very steep, mainly uphill, we'd need to be prepared. After breakfast and packing though, just before we set off, we were to be properly introduced to our support team.

So we found ourselves, breakfast done, rucksacks packed, water bottles filled, waterproofs on, standing outside in a circle with Tony, Paco and the team of eight. Tony explained that they hire men from the local villages we were passing by to help with our trek through their area. It gave them the chance to earn a rare and much needed extra income. They lived with their families in the clay and wattle houses dotted around. Though these looked scattered and isolated to us there were different communities in various parts of the mountains. They were also helping by loaning us the horses that were carrying the equipment, as well as setting up the campsites and taking it down.

We stood in a circle facing each other. On one side a line of many layered, loud, laughing ladies and on the other shy looking, almost bashful men in vivid multi-coloured clothes and hats. Paco stood like a conductor in the middle, translating as we introduced ourselves and said how old we were, what we did, who we lived with. It could have been some strange open air multi-lingual speed dating set up.

These practical men blended fashions Peruvian style, each was wearing jeans or jogging bottoms, their tops covered with their handwoven ponchos. The ponchos, made of thick material, were mainly red with multi coloured tassles dangling all the way round the bottom. They're an important garment for identification not just warmth as each district has its own distinctive localised designs woven into the poncho. The ponchos looked so stiff across the shoulders they seemed like they were held up with coat hangers as the men's arms dangled underneath them.

Rather than the chullos, the knitted hats with ear flaps that are so prevalent, they wore sombrero style felt hats with wide ornate straps under the chin, keeping it in place. Flowing from the top were more multi coloured tassels. The group of men all looked of a similar age - but that could've been anything between 20 to 50.

There was some swaying about, nudging each other and bashful smiles as Paco went round the group - we were told that they were actually of varying ages between 20 and 50, mostly married - although, said Paco with a wink, here all you and the girl have to do is tell people you are married and that is it, there's nothing more to it. All were farmers, having lived in the mountains all their lives, growing crops like potatoes and grains and looking after alpacas. Our jobs probably didn't translate quite as easily and whether they thought it odd that so many of us weren't married - or had been married several times - we never found out.

Some of the crew were more reluctant than others to speak and grinned shyly as we cheered them on. The biggest round of applause - and most sympathetic noises - was for the young man who told us he was responsible for our toilets.

While we were doing our introductions it had started drizzling, grey clouds floated low all around us. By the time we set off we had to wrap ourselves and our rucksacks up in garish waterproof coverings against the persistent wetness. Now I felt like I was 'proper trekking', whatever that was. Here I was in full waterproof clothing, in the middle of remote mountains few people came to, entering a whole different world. It was a very still quiet world, there was no bird song, no road noise, no mechanical sounds at all. The loudest noises came from us. As we climbed a steep barely there path, the noise of our breathing was loud and laboured. I was taking short videos and when I played some of them back the heavy breathing sounded like it should be on an x-rated film, not an innocent walk.

We were also joined by the hardy mountain ponies who followed us, carrying the equipment. None were on ropes or reins, they were an established herd with the lead horse keeping pace with their owner and the rest of them following. Not one strayed, tripped or stopped, sure footed and sure of where they were going. "These are our vehicles now," Paco said. "Nothing can get up here. But if needed the horses can carry people as well as equipment."

It was a sobering thought, I was curious. "So if one of us fell or broke a bone or was taken seriously ill - what would happen, is there a helicopter that would come?"

"No, no helicopter. You would get on an emergency horse and have to go back the way we came." Middle of nowhere, up at high altitude, days from a hospital, with just an emergency horse as the fall back plan - no mountain rescue or flying ambulance here. It would probably be best not to get ill or have an accident here then.

Some others in the group were starting to feel the affects of the altitude or the dreaded Inca Two Step and Suzanne in particular was suffering on this morning. Our little gang at the back that had formed the day before stuck together. Andrea was nominated pace setter, after it was obvious her natural pace was much better than my tendency to speed up if I was in the front.

We fell into a comfortable raggedy line, with Suzanne hanging back to do what she had to do. The trail we were following was wrapped around the side of the mountain. It was scattered with stones and rocks which made it slippery and we had to focus on where to put our feet. We came up with a chant of 'in through the nose and out through the mouth' to help remind us to keep taking deep intakes of breath. This altitude really is something I thought, when we have to remind ourselves how to walk and breathe. I pondered on the things you take for granted... breathing, flushing toilets, walking, running water.

We hadn't travelled very far distance wise but were climbing very high, very quickly. Looking behind us and below I could see the site we'd camped getting more distant. It was stunning, set deep in a valley with a river snaking its way in between the mountains rising up on either side. A grey wet mist swirled up from the bottom of the valley and thickened into clouds. We must have been walking through these as when I looked around clouds were hovering below us, covering much of the surrounding mountains.

It seemed to take a long time to get to anywhere - every time I thought I saw the top we reached it, then saw we still had further to climb. Slow steps were interspersed with stops for drinks, photos, peeing, a snack, a general catch of breath and chat. We finally all caught up as a group when we did reach a ledge that looked like it was going to flatten out. We all stopped, sharing chocolate and drinks and checked how everyone was doing.

The mountain opposite us seemed to stretch up so high but we were up there with it. I looked down, deciding we had definitely climbed an impressive height. There were mountains all around folding into each other but none of them seemed to be taller than where we were currently standing. It felt very much like the top of the world. The colours were all subdued. There were no trees, flowers or anything growing vertically, just mossy, stunted grass scattered with rocks of various grey shades.

We carried on onwards and upwards until there was relief when we realised we had in fact reached perhaps not 'the' top but a top all the same. The land flattened out a bit, giving us the chance to both breathe and speak while we walked. There were outbursts of yodelling and songs and more chattering as we literally got our breath back. Spurring us on was the promise that at some point soon we would actually go down hill.

Tony had told us about the route we'd be taking for the day and described having lunch by a lake. All of a sudden I was looking down and could see in the distance a glistening pool of water and a dark green shade that could be only be our dining tent down below. I let a cheer out as the others came to stand on the edge and looked down with me. "That's where we're heading - that must be it, not far now." Any fancy ideas I'd entertained of sitting by a picturesque lake, resting, soaking up a bit of sun and writing in my journal went right out of my head. The rain hardened and the ground grew even soggier the nearer we got to the lunch stop.

Our incredible crew, who had stayed back after we'd set off to pack everything up, had managed to somehow overtake us, laden down with their loads, reach the lake, set up the kitchen, dining tent and toilets, and have a cooked three course lunch almost ready by the time we got there. How they did it was as amazing and mysterious as the mountains themselves. Were we really that slow..?

8 Ups and Downs

'One climbs, one sees, one descends, one sees no longer but one has seen.' Zene Daumal

Even before we knew their names, marital status and ages, we were being well looked after by our Peru crew. For many of us, used to being the ones in charge at home or work, usually having responsibility for organising other people and multi-tasking, it was a radical change. With my altitude addled brain, not having to plan, prepare or be responsible for anything more than unpacking and re-packing a rucksack was actually quite a relief.

Arriving at our canvas cafe, lunch was a welcome rest and a chance to restock the easily depleted energy levels. The guides sat on the end of the long table, making sure we were all served before tucking in themselves. Appetites seemed to be being affected by the altitude, apart from Paco's. He cleared his plate and was happy for us to hand him anything that was going to be left over and he cleared that too. Whether it was just his way or part of the hierarchy of the crew, he barked orders at Chef when we asked for refills of drinks or anything else. We started joking with him that he should be polite and say please. Paco grinned when there was a loud chorus of 'por favour' from us every time he spoke to the crew after that.

Tony, ever professional, attempted over lunch to explain where we were heading. I did my best to concentrate but to me it sounded like it was to be 'over that mountain there, up, round, up and down'. We were currently in a low bit, we'd climb up again a bit, but nothing like the morning's exertions, then we'd go much further down into a valley to camp for the night. I have been known to get lost in a car park let along up a mountain range so I was full of admiration. Here we were, in the middle of quite frankly identical looking mountains, with no paths, tracks or obvious signposts or landmarks, yet these guides knew exactly where we were going and how to get there.

After lunch, as at every pit stop, there was a debate about waterproofs, clothing and numbers of layers. Despite waterproofs still being advised as the drizzle was unrelenting and things got soaked quickly through, I quickly warmed up while walking so settled for only a t-shirt on underneath a jacket. The dilemma was how quickly I got cold when we stopped for even just a few minutes. Things were shoved in and out of rucksacks until Tony, with his worried smile, said we'd have to set off or we'd be running late. He managed to get us all on the road again- though actually there wasn't even a track let alone a road.

The landscape we were walking through reminded me of models my brother used to make when we were little for his toy soldiers. Landscapes with papier mache Blue Peter style mountains, painted mossy green and covered in hundreds of tiny green filings that created a rough covering, with the occasional pan scourer cut up for a bush effect.

After another couple of hours of laborious walking a cheer went up at the front, echoing back to those of us bringing up the rear. It took our little group at the back a few more minutes to be able to see the sight that had provoked the joy.

We stood on a ridge looking down into a valley, the bottoms of the mountains flowing into each other. There was a silver sliver of river running along and, just in sight near it, was a collection of light green dots. The green was so unlike all of the natural shades of green on the landscape that they stuck out like beacons - our tents!

We now just had to negotiate getting down the very steep, at times almost sheer drop that took us from where we were to where we wanted to be. I was finding that in the Andes when I could see something that appeared to be within reachable distance - actually getting to it seemed to take a lot longer than it should. It was like someone kept moving the end point. So it was with this.

Being able to see the tents was a welcome boost but going down such a steep mountain side was almost trickier than climbing upwards. The shingly ground meant it was easy to slip and slide and though the quickest way was straight down, that would guarantee broken bones, if not death. Even the emergency horses had slowed down and were picking their way carefully. The only way to do it was by taking a long winding zig zag route - probably five times the distance but a hundred times safer. Using walking sticks, hands, rocks and whatever else was handy to grab onto we manoeuvred our way down, turning back on ourselves several times. I occasionally glimpsed up to check that the tents weren't disappearing into the distance like some mirage.

It was around mid afternoon and, though there was still damp clinging in the air, the sky was now blue and when the sun appeared the heat was intense. I couldn't wait to reach camp, not just to rest but because I thought I may get a couple of hours to do my own thing- wander along the river the tents were pitched by, take my journal, sit and write. We carefully and slowly made our way down. The rest of the group were already mingling in and out of tents, carrying bags, refilling water bottles, standing around chatting. Approaching the green row of tents I saw numerous flashes of that unmistakable red. Sitting around in semi circles in front of the tents like an anticipative audience were groups of local women and children.

Claire waved at me from a nearby tent she was perched outside with a bowl of water and I sat down with a thump. She welcomed me with the news that the children had already had sweets, she had mud packs for our feet and that we should be able to get a cup of tea very shortly. I smiled at all of this as I pulled off my rucksack and wondered what to do first. Sit down, take off boots, smother feet in the mud pack, and chat I decided were the best options.

In front of the tent was a row of children sitting to the right. Half a dozen women were sitting with more children and their collection of goods further down the field, then to the left were two more groups of children. Occasionally one or two would catch my eye and then quickly look away. Some were quietly talking or showing each other what goodies they'd got from us - pens, pencils, paper, sweets and balloons. But there was no shouting, or screaming, there was very little noise for the number of children around us. "They look so serious," I said. "They look so muddy," said Claire, "Their feet are covered. And here we are putting on a mud pack from a tube on ours,"

Children and adults wore the same kind of thick strapped rubber looking sandals which I found out are made out of recycling old tyres. The children dressed just like the grown ups. The girls had the same colourful puffy skirts that can be layered up. Around their shoulders was wrapped a handwoven, patterned wrap called an lliclla, knotted or fastened at the front with a pin. The hats, or monteras, they wore vary in style from community to community.

Apparently it's possible to identify the village a woman comes from by the style of her hat. The women and girls here wore similar ones secured with wide woven straps. The boys had the same traditional modern trousers and poncho combination as our support crew had, just a couple of them wore baseball caps rather than the traditional wide brimmed hats.

I wandered over to the ladies sitting so patiently with their goods for sale. They had variations on the same theme, all handmade, rainbow coloured socks, purses, bags, rugs, hats. "Where do they usually sell all these?" I asked Paco. "This isn't a well used tourist trail, they mustn't get many visitors like us coming here." "At the markets," he replied. "They take their goods and walk for sometimes days to get there and back."

We gathered in our canvas cafe to have a much needed cup of tea, catching up with each other. Someone had explored the riverside and reported that it was in fact far too boggy and muddy to get near the river, scuppering my thoughts of a walk along it before dinner.

At the other end of the table to me the discussion had turned to organising the collection for tips for the crew and when to hand them out. Tony explained what usually happened and that the different jobs the men did normally meant a sliding scale of tips, but that it was of course up to us. Also, he patiently explained, giving out the tips was always done in the morning as that would be the last day of the crew being together. He said it would mean us getting away a little bit later or being up a bit earlier to hand the tips out in the morning. In answer to someone's suggestion he said if we really wanted to do it tonight after dinner it was up to us, and his worried smile appeared.

The noise levels rose as a small group took charge, working out who would get what and how much we all needed to put in. I started to remind them that Tony said Doctor would be staying with us so didn't need to be included in this tip money but it was more of an effort trying to get heard than I could make. I took myself back to the tent. It had started to rain and, as I could feel myself flagging, I cancelled my plans to wander off by myself and thought a lie down may be best instead.

Claire came in and sat down in the tent, reporting some disagreement that was occurring over the plans for tipping. We agreed to leave others to it to sort and just put in whatever we were asked for and instead spent a very amicable hour or so in our tent. Rose came in to join us and we were soon exchanging tales of life, love and everything in between. It was the first time I'd really had chance to have any sort of lengthy chat with Claire and she was admirably honest and hysterically funny. I looked outside to check if it was still raining. It was but the children and women were still sitting, seemingly oblivious to the rain, cold and incoming clouds. I heard giggling from the nearest group as the tent's zip made a noise, I waved and ducked back inside.

By the time we'd sorted clothes, bags and 'washed' it was time to take up positions in the dining tent. I was starting to adjust quite nicely to not even having to think about what I was going to have, just wait for it to be served and eat up. Tonight's main dish for us veggies was a delicious spicy pumpkin stew. When we'd finished eating, the crew were called and squashed into one end of the long tent. The decision to hand out the tips after dinner instead of the morning had obviously been made. In dim candle light all of the crew crowded in and were individually thanked for their part in taking care of us. Different members of the group gave each of them their well earned tip money. I hoped they remembered that we were still dependent on them tomorrow until after lunch time.

Claire and I decided to 'go' for the last time before bed behind a wall on the way back to the tent, to avoid the increasingly aromatic toilets. I looked up as we squatted down. In the inky night sky the stars were clearer and more numerous than I'd ever seen. I wished I was better at recognising them. I know the obvious names - the plough, the great bear - but struggle to join them like dot to dots into the right shapes. "This is beautiful. We do have loos with the best views ever." I wondered what the women and children who'd surrounded us before were now doing. Presumably they were asleep in the houses that we'd seen just further down from our camp site. I guessed they'd wake with the sun rise. Get up with the sunlight, go to bed when it gets dark. What could be more natural. Who on earth invented alarm clocks?

As we climbed into our sleeping bags, again too worn out to say much more than good night to each other another thought struck me.
"Do you know Claire - I've not been yet."
"Not been where?"
"You know 'been' been. I haven't yet had a poo in Peru."
It really wasn't that funny, but I blame the effects of tiredness and the altitude for making it seem hilarious at the time. We both cracked up laughing and I went to sleep still giggling.

9 Spirit of the Andes

'The Incas worshipped many gods and believed there was a god for every aspect of the earth, such as the sun, moon, wind, lightening, rain...' Peru Facts

I could feel my eyes were open but I couldn't see anything. The silence was punctuated with rustling noises, and the sound of someone closing up their tent. I was reluctant to move from my cosy cocoon but my stomach told me me I needed to. I reckoned I was going to have another first in Peru.

Grabbing my jacket and torch I slithered to the bottom of the tent to unzip it and put my boots on outside. I could make out just enough in the darkness to guide me towards the toilet area. I pulled my jacket collar up to cover my nose, wondering for a moment if I could just go outside. No, I decided I had to brave the noxious smelling cubicles and braced myself to hold my breath for as long as I could while I was in there.

On my way back to the tent I could make out shadowy figures moving in the distance but couldn't see who it might be. The darkness was eerie and chilly. Back inside Claire momentarily woke up and offered her congratulations when I explained that I had finally 'been'. Relieved to discover after nearly five days that my bodily functions were all still functioning I fell back to sleep. It was still completely dark when I woke up again. I heard an increasingly loud gurgling noise and realised it was coming from my stomach.

Knowing I had to go for a repeat performance I guessed it was just needed after the past few days moratorium. But after a couple more hours and increasingly regular trips, it was obviously it was a bit more than just normal functions returning.

Claire woke as I could hear the low murmurs of the crew bringing our tea and water bowls. "Morning, how are you?" she asked. "Hmm not so good, I reckon I've got the Inca Two Step.' I emerged from the tent, stretching, and Rose appeared. She'd also had a sleepless night, suffering from the same thing as me.

I decided to skip breakfast, take the maximum amount of Imodium and have a supply handy to keep taking it until it worked. Rose went to see the Doctor, delicately explaining with accompanying visual signs, what was wrong. He nodded understandingly and handed her a tablet. We couldn't quite work out exactly what the big brown lozenge was but it was seemingly the answer to any and all ills. I turned down the offer of this medication, explaining I'd already taken Imodium so would be fine.

My only concern was to make sure it didn't happen when I was walking, especially as this was the day we were tackling the longest section of the trek. No amount of toilet tissues, wet wipes and sympathy from others could help in that situation. Terrified of the Imodium not working, I borrowed the largest sanitary pad available for extra safety and felt like I was wearing a nappy. At least mountain trek fashion included baggy trousers with plenty of room in them.

It really struck home that no matter how tired or poorly any of us felt, not going on just wasn't an option. As well as having a bad night's sleep and the same tummy trouble as me, Rose's knee was playing up too and she was feeling tired and teary. Faye's bad back was, well, bad and she felt she was struggling. As the others set off our at-the-back group tried to rally each other.

The only Plan B we had was a group hug and utilising the emergency horses. Faye's and Rose's backpacks were piled up on one and Faye piled onto another. Rose strapped her knee up and felt more confident about walking without her rucksack. She agreed to see how she got on, with the back up plan of also getting on horse back if needed.

The mood lifted and, shuffling, rustling, smiling again, we set off on the longest part of the trek.

We were straightaway climbing steeply again, out of the valley we'd slept in and up the almost vertical sides of the surrounding mountain. As I looked down I realised what hadn't been apparent the previous night was that we had been in the perimeter of a relatively large settlement. Around 30 houses sat either side of the river, each surrounded by a stone wall marking the land belonging to that property. The clay walled houses were a simple rectangle topped with a grassy thatched roof, that dangled over the edges like a long fringe. Tony's plan to take us to see inside a house yesterday had been scuppered by the residents not being in. But he'd explained that inside is just one room, usually smoke filled as there's a fire in the centre of the house for cooking and warmth, but no chimney. All different generations of the family live together, with guinea pigs scuttling around the earth floors, just feet away from their final destination - the cooking pot.

The early morning clouds were lifting from the ground, revealing the mountains around us. We all soon stripped off our jackets and fleeces as the heat intensified. As we reached a plateau a handful of children appeared, scampering around with just a dog for company. They grinned and ran ahead of us, waited until we'd caught up then ran off again.

People seemed to appear out of thin air and then just disappear again like some kind of mountain magic. The energy they had gave such a contrast to our lack in that department. They walked quickly, or ran, everywhere. We rarely saw even horses being used. This way of life is almost unchanged from hundreds of years ago. We were debating whether we could live with the lack of possessions, tools and technology, just having self sufficiency and reliance on each other. To some of us a more simple way of life appealed - make and grow what you can, take things to sell where and when you can. If you want to get somewhere, walk yourself there. But of course apparent simplicity and freedom comes with unfamiliar hardships. I was already looking forward to a hot shower and charging my phone up. so maybe not the life for me. But still, I mused, there was something very special here.

We were brought out of philosophical ramblings by the sudden appearance of a curly haired black dog running towards us. Except as it came nearer is was obviously not a dog but a sheep. It had darted out from a stone house that stood completely on its own, with just the mountains for neighbours. Unlike normal sheep behaviour, to turn tail and run from anything and everything, this one hurtled up to us and stood fearlessly facing us. I'm sure if it could speak it would have asked us what on earth we thought we were doing on his land.

A gap toothed lady appeared from the house clutching the hand of a child so small he looked like he shouldn't yet be walking. With a wide grin she came up to us now crowded round the sheep, who was more than happy to be petted and fussed. She smiled and exchanged words with Paco. As she was talking to him, the sheep took a liking to Paco, head butting his leg. When a couple of dogs appeared it lost interest in him and decided to say hello to his fellow creatures.

"This sheep," Paco said,"is a family pet. He has been brought up in the house like a pet. He actually thinks he is a dog." As he spoke, the sheep demonstrated his personality confusion. He was sniffing around the dogs and when a little puppy tried to bite his nose he gently head butted him so he stopped. We watched fascinated and amused. I'd noticed that there seemed to be a lot of dogs around but not working dogs to help the farmers, they just seemed to be pets.

As we started to climb again, the barely there track we had been following disappeared and the ground turned rocky. Rose decided to have a break and use the emergency horse, though having watched Fay clinging on for dear life as her horse took great big leaps over stones and puddles it looked like it would be more hair raising than relaxing.

We were going up again as the increasing breathlessness told us if we needed evidence, climbing out of a shallow valley. In front of us the bottom of the mountains at either side blended smoothly into the landscape where the two met. It looked like someone had taken a giant ice cream scoop and just used it to shape out the valley in the middle. The clouds hung around like misty shrouds. It looked like they were getting lower when in fact we were of course climbing higher.

Among the Quechan people, religious beliefs - although blended with Catholicism and other Christian elements - are still largely traditional from Inca times. Pachamama - Mother Earth - is particularly revered, with offerings regularly made to her and out here it is easy to understand why. Also of importance to the Andean people are the mountain spirits known as apu. As I stopped to admire the clouds and commented on the awe inspiring scenery Paco explained that the clouds are also thought of as spirits and the streams that appear trickling through the mountains are their tears.

We were walking on a relatively flat level with a clear view for miles in front, the same barren landscape stretching ahead. We hadn't passed or seen a house for some time so it was a surprise when we came across two ladies with a small child sat on the ground. They looked for all the world like they had just stopped to have a picnic at their favourite spot. But instead of a picnic basket, sandwiches and cake, in front of them spread out on a k'eperina were materials in bright reds, yellows and oranges. Somehow they had known we were on our way. Obviously not wanting to miss an opportunity they'd come out here with their wares. Who needs mobile phones when you have a mountain grapevine like that.

They were selling colourful hand woven cloth, all different shapes and sizes. Handmade items probably made for their own use, for clothing or to carry things in, could also handily double up as potential sales to visitors. I spotted a large piece of cloth that looked intricate and beautifully woven. I asked Paco to interpret knowing it wasn't even worth me trying to ask. He gave me a price that I thought was fair but he said it was too much and negotiated it down. Eventually I paid the equivalent of about £25 for my very own piece of Quechan craftsmanship. I still thought it was a bargain. Paco called it a 'fair' price. I picked up the cloth, which smelt heavily of smoke and had a smattering of mud on it. Paco folded it up and put it in one of the bags he was carrying as it was too big to go into my rucksack and we set off again, waving goodbye to the two ladies.

Further on, with everyone else trooping ahead, a couple of us hung back in need of a toilet stop. It was now so natural to just squat down wherever and whenever needed, with no shelter, that I did wonder whether we'd have to stop ourselves doing this when we got back to 'civilisation'. As we stood up there was the familiar red flash on the horizon, the colours standing out among the muted mountains. When the figure came closer I recognised her as the older grey haired lady who had been sitting with the one I'd bought my material from.

We'd now fallen quite far back from the others including the guides. We could see in the vast landscape ahead dots appearing then disappearing again as the rest of the group moved over the undulating terrain. We moved on slowly, picking our way carefully over the ground that was both boggy and rocky.

Our Peruvian friend slowed down a bit as she caught up with us, and then carried on walking at a slight distance to our right. She regularly glanced across and smiled at us, stopping and waiting for us to catch up if we dropped behind. Along the marshy ground there were narrow rivers to cross and she trotted ahead, leading us over rocks hidden in the shallow parts. It was like having our very own guardian apu. When we caught up with the others, who had stopped for a rest, we told them about our personal guide. I looked around for her but she'd gone.

After a surge of effort needed to get up a long steep climb, we were finally headed slightly downward towards the welcome sight of the dining tent. The going was getting tougher as the ground grew increasingly soggy from the now constant drizzle. By the time we reached the canvas cafe I was feeling chilled through. We kept most of our gear on, dripping and cold, waterproofs rustling with every movement.

Though the Imodium seemed to be working I didn't want to risk a repeat performance of the Inca Two Step so to Paco's delight I passed him my plate that had been filled with Chef's freshly cooked veggie dish. I sucked on a piece of chocolate to pacify Tony who was issuing 'you must eat' advice with his concerned look. I was happy just to have a hot drink as I was starting to feel even colder now I'd stopped moving.

By the time we set off again it was raining heavily. Inevitably we were heading upwards, the soft ground squelching under our footsteps. The regular members of our group at the back were joined by others at various times except for the hard core at the front who just disappeared at their own pace. Claire joined us now and so did Jane and Sally, who I hadn't really yet had a chance to speak to much. We were spending 24 hours a day together yet there were still some of the group I hadn't got to really know. Walking so spread out, sitting at the long thin dining tables and then crashing out early didn't leave a lot of time or energy for socialising.

As the afternoon went on there was relief when the land flattened out but effort was then refocused on the hazardous terrain. As well as having to avoid bits too boggy to walk over, we had to navigate streams flowing through the mossy undergrowth and the constant uneven rockiness that tripped several people up, including Paco who took a tumble.

Though wet and weary, as we weren't climbing up so steeply as before we had more opportunity to talk as we walked. We compared our mountain chic wear, with Claire undoubtedly the winner in the trekking fashion stakes. She was wearing a massive waterproof cape that looked like a bin bag and drowned her five foot frame. It also covered her rucksack and, with just head and arms sticking out, made her look like the hunchback of Notre Dam. At one point as the conversation somehow turned to dancing she decided to give a demonstration, choosing a slightly bewildered Doctor as her partner. One moment he was quietly walking with us, struggling with the conversation, then the next he was twirled into tangoing with a slightly crazed Englishwoman on a soaking wet mountainside. We blamed the altitude.

The rain and mist made the remote landscape increasingly bleak. After many miles without a sign of any life at all a stone building came into view. In front of it, in a square plot that had been walled off, were neatly planted rows of potatoes. It was a slightly surreal sight.

The group was spread out but we were close enough to the others to see them pointing ahead. I looked across and could just make out something a little further on that looked like a path. As we got closer we realised it was more than a path - it was a road, stony, rocky Peruvian style of course - but a road. We still seemed to be in the middle of nowhere, but we must be nearly somewhere.

We headed towards it, picking our way carefully down a sloping side, across another river, than climbed up until we reached it and felt the joy of solid stone beneath our feet. Gathered on the empty road, we were faciing a spectacular view of a valley in front cutting through snow topped mountains. Tony was pointing out something in the distance, a small rectangular shape sitting on the road. It was our coach waiting for us. There were two options to reach it. We could follow the road curving round the mountain. It looked like quite a long way to get there but it would be on the flat solid path. Or go back downhill, into the bogginess below, make our way across more marsh land, cross another river, and climb up another steep incline. In theory shorter but more of a challenge. The decision was made for us - of course we would take the latter route.

Weary and wet through, knowing we were so close brought a bit of a boost to flagging energy. In the true vein of the trek it of course took longer than it looked to get there. Eventually we negotiated one last river, helping each other across the slippery stones, clambered up the final climb and reached the coach, an odd sight parked on a deserted road in the middle of a mountain.

As ever I was among the last on board, grateful to just collapse into a seat. So tired that even when the message filtered back that the bus driver had had difficulty getting here I didn't really take any notice. There had been landslides so bad due to the rain that parts of the road were almost impassable. The driver knew if he hadn't come to pick us up we would have been stuck. He had to negotiate with officials and risk driving on a route deemed so dangerous even to locals that it had actually been closed. This was the road we were now heading on to our next stop.

10 Into the Valley

'Stop worrying about the potholes in the road and celebrate the journey.' Fitzhugh Mullan

I hadn't seen much evidence on the trip that the Peruvians are particularly concerned about health and safety. Yet the road we now had to travel on had been deemed so dangerous in the current conditions that it had been officially closed. But there was no other way of getting out or going onwards. Our wily driver had managed to 'persuade' the authorities to let him and our coach through and he had made it to our meeting point. So it couldn't be too bad - surely...

As the bus set off however, filling up with the smell of damp clothing and noise of chatter, it quickly became obvious why it was closed. We were heading downwards, the narrow road clinging to the side of the mountains, on an already heart in mouth route that had become more treacherous in the heavy rain.

At increasingly regular intervals there were rocks on the narrow road of various sizes. The biggest landslides meant that the driver had to slowly inch his way around, getting precariously nearer to the edge and the sheer drop below. At times where there were smaller rocks or it seemed that squeezing past would be impossible the bus had to just go over the top of them. Presumably as it was still raining, there was also the possibility of further landslides happening and our bus was pretty much a sitting (or crawling) target. We were suddenly quiet, all appreciating the seriousness of it, it was hard not to when you could see it in front and to the sides of you out of the windows.

For the first time on the trip I felt really worried, recalling stories I occasionally read in the press about buses crashing abroad - is this what it feels like, what actually happens, who on earth would find us out here? I closed my eyes and decided if I couldn't sleep then at least pretending to would help - like putting your head under a pillow when you're little to hide from scary monsters. I could feel the twists and turns of the bus and hearing the regular gasps and comments from the others gave me all the information I needed.

After what felt like a lifetime I opened my eyes as the road levelled and widened out, we were down from the mountains and into a valley. The relief this brought was short lived as we were driving alongside a gushing river, swollen and angry with the recent rain, that at regular intervals had burst its banks, spilling its water over the road. The bus turned from mountaineer to amphibian as we drove through floods, until finally we headed away from the river, to dry land and signs of life.

The landscape was altering, leaving behind the bare beauty and bleakness of the mountains we'd been in. Greenery and trees started appearing, occasionally a house, then a few more, then some advertising hoardings, paths next to the road, further on people sitting around and walking, then we passed through a small town. Bit by bit signs of development and modern day life appeared.

As we approached the town of Ollantaytambo it was getting dark. We were greeted by sights that felt strangely unfamiliar - lights, people, a couple of cars. The coach pulled up in the middle of the town, outside a hotel. After cheering the driver for his amazing skills and ability to get us there safely, we clambered off the bus. I looked around, the scene reminded me of the old cowboy films my dad used to watch.

Across the dusty main road from the hotel, was a row of squat stone buildings with wooden balconies and shutters, thatched awnings with a few chairs and tables under them. On the film sets of course they only built the front of the buildings, with nothing behind. I crossed the road and looked through a couple of the open doors - there was a shop, people buying things - a restaurant, people eating inside, sitting at tables. I couldn't believe how alien it felt - had we really only been in the mountains for a couple of nights?

I realised everyone else had disappeared into the hotel and went to join them. Rose, Claire and I had decided to share a room and they were already at the reception desk negotiating a key. Our party filled the small entrance lobby with our damp clothes aroma, rucksacks, bags and noise.

After some confusion, as originally others had been given the only triple room, we made our way inside and up to our room. Past the reception area, the hotel was built around a roofless courtyard in the middle, complete with pond and plants, the balconies covered in climbing vines. It was definitely bringing the outside in. As with all buildings, it was built low and we climbed the single set of stairs to our room. Although tired from the day's trek, we were obviously at a lower altitude because just going upstairs felt easier than before.

The hotel with its wood and exposed brickwork looked traditionally built but actually wasn't very old. It certainly felt safe, welcoming - and clean, which was more then we were. We found our long spacious room, with three beds in a row. I fell onto one with a grateful moan. A soft mattress, pillows, clean sheets - this was heavenly, I didn't want to move. But we had a schedule to stick to of course - three women, one bathroom, several bags, and less than an hour to get changed and go out again.

As I lay unmoving, Claire and Rose were into full getting organised mode. Number one priority was to utilise every plug socket we could fine - phone chargers went on and Claire found her hairdryer and straighteners. Rose went into the shower first and came out wrapped in towels, reporting back with a happy sigh "it's warm and I am clean". Claire opted to shower next, leaving me working out yet again what items were going to go into which bag. We heard a shriek and she came out clutching her towel around her. "It's freezing cold!" she said, "We can't shower in that." As the only one fully clothed I went downstairs to reception and bumped into a handful of others also doing the same - and not just from our group. I tried not to feel guilty as the hot water shortage could well have been something to do with the sudden influx of 15 scruffy trekkers all trying to use it at the same time. The girl and boy behind the desk who looked like young backpackers themselves promised to sort it out. "Hot will be back in five minutes," they said confidently.

Back in the room after 15 minutes it was still what could be at best described as lukewarm. But time was getting on so we decided not very warm running water was better than we'd had for a while. Although we didn't have long, just being somewhere comfortable felt slightly relaxing. Rose and I were having a discussion about post cancer reconstruction, when Claire stepped out of the bathroom. Rose was in the middle of baring all to show me her surgeon's handiwork. Claire walked up to us, having missed the conversation. "Are we flashing?" she asked and, without waiting for an answer dropped her towel. We collapsed into a heap of giggles - and of course blamed the altitude.

Despite the tepid shower, having running water, soap and shampoo, replacing damp dirty smelly clothes with clean ones was bliss. We were just about on time to meet everyone else downstairs, last ones as was now usual. I was still not very hungry and did think I'd quite like just to mooch around here on my own or with my room buddies. But I reminded myself I was part of a group, with a schedule to stick to and I definitely wouldn't have wanted to give Tony any more worries as he was doing such a sterling job keeping us all on track. So we set off en masse, out of Hotel Sol, which we wouldn't actually get to see in the daylight.

I didn't realise until I looked it up back home that the hotel was built next to the river flowing alongside the town, the Patacancha. On the other side of the hotel the rooms have balconies overlooking the impressive Inca ruins, which we only glimpsed as we walked past, with their huge perfect stones and stepped grassy terraces.

Ollantaytambo has been an important historical site, in the 15th century conquered and rebuilt by Inca emperor Pachacuti, then later a base for Manoc Inca, leader of the resistance against the Spanish conquest. In more recent times, 19th century explorers flocked here attracted by the prime example of Inca ruins. Today, it's a popular starting point for people trekking the traditional Inca trail or, with its station, taking the train to Machu Picchu. Having not had the chance to explore, it is definitely another place I'd like to go back and spend more time in.

We walked past tuk tuks, dogs, stalls with food, gifts and clothing. Although bustling compared to where we'd been to, it still felt like a relatively small town.

We passed a few cosy looking restaurants but kept walking until we came to the end of the road. Although I knew we'd be getting a train from here it was still a shock to see something as formal as a sign and a proper looking train station. We stopped short of actually going onto the station platform and instead turned into a restaurant next to it. It was part of a hotel called Alberque, the sign outside stating that the proprietor is one Wendy Weeks.

I wasn't really hungry but realising it was 24 hours since I had last eaten properly had some pasta. I usually love food to it was an unusual experience for me to eat for the sake of having to, rather than to enjoy it. The early mornings and long days trekking were taking their toll on everyone. Apart the obligatory pisco sour, we stuck to soft drinks and everyone was ready to head straight back to our hotel after the meal. As we walked back, around us there were signs that the evening wasn't yet over for others. We paused to buy water from the shop opposite the hotel, Paco stayed outside chatting to people and looked like he may be set for a night out without us.

As we collapsed into our beds in our triple room, Rose, Claire and I carried on talking. Chatting plus the novelty of being able to send text messages, check FaceBook and post photos meant that by the time we switched the lights off there was less than six hours to go before we were on our way again. Not getting much sleep had just become the norm.

In the morning, as our three alarms went off simultaneously, it seemed to take some effort to get my tired limbs moving. Thankful that we'd done most of our packing the night before, Rose, Claire and I negotiated the bathroom and joined the others for breakfast. There was very little time and not being at all hungry I made do with a cup of coca tea. How quickly this earthy tasting drink had gone up in my estimation. I now actually looked forward to it and preferred it to the coffee.

In spite of the lack of sleep and ungodly hour, I reckoned the lower altitude must be having a positive effect on me. I was feeling better than I had all week. Was this the extra oxygen working its silent magic? I couldn't help exclaiming how good I was feeling to anyone in the vicinity and, given the early hour and bleary eyes, really wouldn't have blamed them if they'd slapped me.

After we'd brought our bags down and checked out, we were handed packed lunches for the day's trek. These were in handmade muslin bags, tied with weaved ribbons in bright reds, greens and oranges. The veggie and gluten free squad were again well catered for. I opened mine up to take a peek – it looked like a sandwich, fruit, cake, chocolate and drink. Even with a packed lunch we were being really well fed.

After the usual last minute hold ups - which went along the lines of someone losing something then somebody else wandering off - Tony, faced fixed into his concerned smile, ushered us out of the hotel, worried that we would miss our train. Light was just starting to yawn its way over the mountains we were surrounded by and the street lights were fading out as we retraced our steps from the previous night.

Enterprising as ever, though it was only 6am, there were already some keen vendors selling woven wares along the street. There were also a few people at the station before us, even keener not to miss the train that was sitting silently at the edge of the platform. I sipped a take away coffee as we were handed out our tickets, then climbed into a carriage pulled by the gleaming engine.

The interior was worthy of all the exclamations it elicited from us. Inca Rail was better than any British Rail experience I've had. We were seated in soft leather luxury seats with polished wooden tables that matched the gleaming wooden floor, surrounded by Inca related murals covering every inch of the walls.

Smiling uniformed staff welcomed us on board. We collectively decided we all wanted a go of the toilet, the obsession with toilets still ongoing. By the time we set off there was already a queue, but it was worth the wait. It was not just clean but gleaming, with not just toilet paper but soft toilet paper, not just flushable but with a gold handle that flushed with gusto. Never have I been more impressed or excited about a toilet.

Staff wearing peaked caps came through with a trolley. We were offered free drinks and selection of snacks, from cheese straws to chocolate cake beautifully wrapped and very tasty. The excitement was finished off with branded Inca Rail chocolates which I shoved in my bag to discover a bit bashed and battered days later, but still edible enough to give to Dylan when I got home.

The 90 minute train journey flew by as we sped through the Sacred Valley. Looking out of the window was like watching a wildlife programme, with a variety of views, snow capped mountains, jungle green forests, roaring rivers. Tony sat at the table opposite, telling us about the landscape and area, pointing out some of the best places for climbing and kayaking. It was also our first chance to have a good chat with another doctor new to the group, who had joined us for the rest of the trip. She spoke perfect English and was keen to find out more about what we were doing the trek for and what had happened so far.

The train slowed then came to a juddery halt. We clambered off at our stop, a wooden platform in the middle of very green, lush surroundings, all except Claire who we had to say a temporary goodbye to. She had booked onto the trek too late in the day to be able to get a pass to go onto this part of the Inca trail. To protect the popular trail the number of visitors allowed to walk it is now limited to 200 a day. Understandably there's a high demand for the passes and by the time she'd booked the company wasn't able to get any more. Instead she was going straight onto Machu Picchu town, Agua Caliente, and being met there by a guide. She was going to join us at the Sun Gate, the entrance we were heading to, in about eight hours time.

The train chugged off on its way, leaving us standing next to a large sign that read 'Camino Sagrado Chacabamba KM 104 Welcome To the Inka Trail'. We made our way onto a rope bridge with wooden slats to get our way across the gushing river. As we stepped on there was another sign overhead declaring Welcome to Inka Trail.

After managing for three days in the middle of remote mountains, seeing signs telling you where you were was a bit odd. This was definitely a different kind of route to the one we'd experienced on the Lares trail. We paused for photos underneath the sign on the bridge before going carefully across one by one. Despite this presumably being now on the 'main trail' the bridge still had a thrown together kind of style. I made my way across it, feeling excitement and energy rising with every wobble. Today finally I'd see Machu Picchu.

11 One step at a time

'It is good to have an end to journey toward; but it is the journey that matters in the end.' Ernest Hemmingway

The change in environment was as welcome to me as the change in the oxygen levels. We were now surrounded by green foliage, huge trees, vines, bird noises. The signs and sounds of life were such a contrast to so the barren mountains of the previous days.

We arrived at some kind of reception area, except that makes it sound a bit grander than it was, there was just a couple of huts – but there was a toilet sign. Still obsessed by the idea of an indoor toilet despite the kind we'd experienced, several of us decided to go one last time before we set off. We were not expecting much and were not disappointed. The door didn't even shut properly, and was too far away to prop shut with your feet as you sat on the loo, so we were all visible to the outside world anyway.

Tony gathered us round and gave instructions for our last trekking day and dealt with our questions- yes there would be insects, lots; yes there could be snakes, perhaps poisonous; and yes there'd be other things that could be dangerous to touch; yes it was jungley - but no, there were not lions or bears.

We'd made such a noxious cloud of industrial strength insect repellant with our enthusiastic spraying, that even if there were lions and bears I felt they would just keel over too. The day was heating up quickly and I could feel the humidity. I shoved the fleece I'd started the day off wearing into my rucksack. I didn't think I'd need it but a company that had kindly donated money to my fundraising had given me it so I'd promised to get photos of it with their logo at Machu Picchu.

We moved off in an aroma of sun tan cream and insect repellant and then regrouped after about ten minutes as we come to a clearing and our first sight of Inca ruins along the Inca Trail. 'Ruins' feels like the wrong word to use about these intriguing sites when they are so intact. The walls and frame of these particular buildings were so perfect it looked like someone was just in the middle of developing an exclusive rural retreat and builders had just downed tools for a break.

As Tony filled us in on the serious stuff about how the buildings were made and used, Paco, ever the comedy element of the duo, lay down on a wall in a series of poses as we took photos. After a final pause for a full group photo, Rosie made a general suggestion that as it was our last day it would be nice to be all together when we finally reached the Sun Gate. Understandably the group had splintered and divided into smaller ones. Along the trek there had tended to be the 'ones in the front' always ahead, not wanting to wait, and the 'ones at the back' the slower, the injured and those not wanting rush. It had been nothing like my worst fears about being with an all female group for such an intense time, with strong characters and a challenging environment though. I was happy with the group of friends I'd made and the pace at the back but Rose had a point that it might be nice to at least cross the finish line together as a whole group.

As we set off I felt like I'd been marooned on another planet for the past few days. I was ridiculously excited to be among greenery, noise and smells, the sun was shining and I was feeling better than I had all week. I dawdled, taking photographs of almost every flower I saw, fascinated by the butterflies and occasional bird overhead. The air was humid, the sun already hot and we were surrounded by scents of trees, flowers and life. I couldn't have been happier.

We'd joined the classic Inca Trail, the one so popular one with tourists that numbers now have to be limited, although there are a number of other options. All, including the Lares Valley route we took, are Inca Trails, and converge eventually to this final part of the adventure. This day would involve climbing stone steps, lots and lots of them, rough slabs cut into the side of the mountains, with a long sheer drop on one side. We debated how many there would be, one suggestion was that there are apparently three thousand steps along this trail. I could believe that but I wasn't going to start counting.

The steps are uneven, different sizes and very narrow in parts, so we often had to walk carefully in single file. Given how small the Inca people were, it is another mysterious oddity as to why they built them quite so large, as in places they looked like steps made for giants. It must have taken a lot of effort to climb them, as we struggled in parts. As is the Peruvian way, there are no fences or barriers to stop you should you stumble and fall, you'd just tumble straight down the side of the mountain to the bottom a long way below.

As we moved onwards and upwards, it was only here, walking precariously on the edge of a mountain, a sheer drop to one side, that I discovered Jane was afraid of heights. It was largely given away by the slightly terrified look on her face and occasional refusal to move. Though I'd only got to know her a little, my impression had been of someone very much in control, independent and strong. I guess that's why these kind of fears are called irrational. It's also something that up there you really have little choice about - there was no going back, she just had to conquer it. I was amazed and full of admiration that she had chosen to do this. I had no idea what this kind of fear is like or what to do, but joined the other girls in gentle encouragement and persuasion when necessary.

It could've been the rush of oxygen into my blood stream or last trek day exuberance but I felt a covered in a blanket of complete happiness and contentment. It was so peaceful, alive, and absolutely stunning. We were climbing up tree covered mountains that rolled into each other, below the Urubamba river glistened at the bottom of the valley, the noise and sight of the occasional train dashing along next to the river getting more distant. We were among the kind of mountains I'd imagined, the type from a child's drawing, green, triangular, pointy topped fairytale mountains stretching into clouds.

As I stopped to put more sun cream on, Paco pointed into the distance – "that's our lunch stop". I strained my eyes and could just about make out a grey scar cut into the dark green side of the mountain. "That's where we've got to get to for lunch?" It looked a long way. "Yes, it's maybe another hour and half." I gathered that the path would follow this mountain around the bend to the left then at some point it would bend to the right and then finally we would get to the little grey spot. "What is it?" "Inca ruins, Winay Wayna, there's many steps but it's very beautiful, we'll eat our lunch sitting up there."

Though I knew we were now on the most popular trail it was still a shock to see other people who were not locals but tourists. There were also occasional shelters where we stopped for short breaks, wooden structures with thatched roofs providing welcome shade, looking over that incredible valley view. Andrea had brought along her stuffed toy Squeaky, who travelled in her rucksack with his head popping out. She was getting some photos of him to show the children back at her nursery, so she could tell them about the Inca trail and his adventures. At one stop Squeaky was positioned daringly on the edge of the shelter to get the amazing view in, causing Andrea worry in case he fell over the edge and was lost for ever. Paco rescued him and gave him mouth to mouth resuscitation, much to the bemusement of a couple of other tourists who passed by at that moment.

As we went on we went deeper into the mountain where there was more shady foliage and the air turned damp, as did the rocks which made them perilously slippery. Cautiously clambering downwards on the steps was actually harder than going up them.

We went carefully one by one over a tiny rope bridge with missing wooden slats that looked like it had been made by boy scouts - ones that hadn't passed their bridge building badge. The noise of water gushing got louder and as we turned another bend there was the source - an enormous waterfall thundering into the river below. While the others picked their way carefully over the stepping stones to the other side, a few of us stopped for photos, looking like we were showering in the waterfall which at this point in time was actually very appealing. The spray from it was a wonderful coolant.

Without quite realising it until we were there, we reached Winay Wayna. We were actually at the bottom of a lot of very steep steps that we had climb up to get the exact spot we were to have our lunch break at. I looked around, wanting to breathe the scenery in, the rich green mountains, tops poking through clouds, and right in front of us ancient stone ruins heaving history and mystery, with alpacas wandering about the ledges. It was obviously their favourite lunch spot too.

I was pleased that my training was finally paying some dividends, though the going was strenuous my legs and lungs were doing fine. It was a relief to know that my struggles on other days really were down to the altitude not fitness. The number and steepness of the steps we now had to climb was challenging at the end of about four hours walking but I did it quite comfortably. Steps I could do - altitude I couldn't.

We finally sat down in a group within a circular wall that looked like it was made for picnics. These ruins were like the others we'd seen, almost complete and really sturdy. There were even window frames which looked out and gave an incredible vantage point of the vista. It was the most scenic picnic spot I've ever been in. It was also the first meal I'd really started to enjoy all week - in the veggie pack there was some kind of pesto sandwich, along with fruit, chocolate, cake and a drink. I tucked in happily, starting to get my appetite back.

When we set off again after a very short rest, I felt refreshed, spurred on knowing that we were now just a few hours from getting 'there'. At one point we carefully picked our way over fallen rocks that made an already narrow path even thinner. Tony stopped. "Here just a few years ago, a guide was killed," he said. "The rain when it falls just causes land slides and here he was standing with a group when a rock loosened by the rain fell and hit him." We speeded up past that point just in case lightening, or in this case falling rock, does strike twice.

Further on we passed some kind of hostel or centre for trekkers who were stopping along the route. Seeing a crowd of young, noisy people was a shock and though there were toilets and we were in need, we just hurried past. Further on when the coast was clear, and there was a little concave shelter in the rock, three of us squatted down overlooking the edge of the mountain, the toilet with the best view in the world.

We fell naturally into our straggly line at the back, enjoying the scenery and company. Andrea and I made up stories about Squeaky's adventures that she could tell the children back home. We weren't in a rush, all of the guides were in front and out of sight with the others. There was no chance of getting lost, with just one direction to go in, one path to follow. Just in case there was any doubt, there was even the odd signpost dotted along the way.

Eventually we caught up with a few of the others standing around at the bottom of what looked like a stone wall. Except it wasn't a wall - it was part of the path but at almost 90 degrees, definitely looked more like a climbing wall. "Really - we go up that?" "Yes, straight up, this is the last fifty steps" grinned Paco, adding kindly, "I'll hold sticks and bags if you like". Looking for where to put hands and feet, grabbing onto the ledges formed by some of the rocks, and with the ones at the top verbally directing others, we eventually all made it up to the top. "Not far now," reassured Paco. "Hey, you said that was the last fifty?!" "Well almost. They were the last very steep ones!"

Ahead we were still climbing upwards, but he was right, the stone path widened out, sloping more gently upwards. I look ahead and realised at the top the girls seemed to be disappearing through a wall. A wall - or a gate? "Are we here, is this it?" It all seemed a bit sudden and unexpected but as I got to the top Claire appeared throwing her arms up with a welcoming hug and squeal, "You made it!"

Still taken aback by the abruptness of arriving, despite having walked towards it for the past eight hours, I realised this actually was the Sun Gate. It did look more like a rocky wall to climb through rather than famed entrance to a mystical paradise.

I walked through, and saw most of the others were already milling around at the other side, having been there for some time. I looked ahead, looking from them to the view in front and saw... nothing but clouds.

12 First sight

'Dreams are the seedlings of realities.' James Allen

"Oh, erm.. where is it?" Having gone through altitude sickness, all weather trekking, nights in cold damp tents, bus rides from hell and a final eight hours trek of continually climbing steps, after finally making it through the legendary Sun Gate the view was a little disappointing to say the least.

Where there should be that iconic view, the one I'd seen and fallen for in the advert, there was just a white out of clouds. They obliterated everything and looked settled, as if they weren't going to move anywhere in a hurry.

"Yes, it is very cloudy but keep watching you'll see it, the clouds blow away," Paco said, seeing my disappointment. He then turned away, resuming his role of group photographer with enthusiasm - particularly when a handful of the girls decided to go for a full charity photo and took their tops off to get snapped in pink bras.

I caught up with some of the others, the peak posse and our gang at the back. We hugged and congratulated each other - we had indeed made it - and took photographs, still with just a cloudy mist in the background. I then decided to call Dylan, as I had promised to ring when I got there. Oddly there is great mobile phone reception at the top of the Sun Gate, unlike on the rest of the trek. (Perhaps this helps give rise to the suggestion the Incas were indeed aliens from a future time...?)

"What can you see?" he asked, when he answered the phone, sounding as clear as if I was ringing from a few miles away. He laughed when I told him just a lot of cloud and we then exchanged brief notes on what we'd been up to - I mentioned I hadn't liked the altitude very much (understatement) but today was great on the last bit, we'd been on a posh train and were now here looking down on a load of cloud and somewhere behind it was Machu Picchu. Usually phone calls to him are short and sweet but he wanted me to hang on and keep talking - I like to think because he was missing me, but it may well have been him just trying to run my bill up.

When we eventually said goodbye and I turned around, the cloud was blowing slowly away, finally bit by bit revealing 'that' view. The one on postcards, in photographs, in books, the one you see on TV. The clouds drifted away as if they'd been part of the deal - teasingly, slowly disappearing to make the moment even more anticipated and drawn out. The sun shone down through the gaps in the clouds looking like beams of light. Being revealed was the grey markings of a settlement carved into the dark green landscape. It looked small and distant but there it was - Machu Picchu.

From the distance it looked like it could be built from Lego, lines of grey bricks set neatly out in well planned formations, like a maze. There were rows of grass topped steps leading down the mountain. Providing the most stunning part of the spectacular back drop was Wayna Picchu, which rises up and looks like it is standing guard over Machu Picchu, the new peak protecting the old.

The Sun Gate, or Inti Punku, is where you can, if you wish, hike to in the dark to watch the sun rise, although from what I've heard it gets quite crowded. It did feel like that whatever time of day this was the only way to arrive and get a first sight of Machu Picchu. When you walk through the stone entrance onto the terrace, like a purpose built viewing platform, you're higher up than Wayna Picchu and have a complete panoramic, breathtaking view. I could have just stood and stared all day.

Our group of 15 females took over at the Sun Gate, ringing home, chatting, hugging, crying, dominating the ledges and edges for photos. Finally we had our last group shots, all of us together, just fitting along the path, still giving Tony things to worry about "Mind the edge... don't step any further back... be careful." Our chorus of 'chi-chiiiis' rang out loudly, shattering any peace and quiet.

We started walking down the well worn path from the Sun Gate - passing a few others going up and others passing us on their way down. I was in my usual position dawdling at the back. The closer we got the more intriguing Machu Picchu looked, the size and scale becoming more obvious. It is a dramatic scene and a stunning setting, and easy to see why this place has the mystical mythical reputation it has.

The walk was all down hill, the path was again on the very edge of the mountain, precarious at times and made more so with distracting views that seemed to get more incredible with every step. As we walked, word was somehow sent back to us that Tony was getting worried that we were late and were going to miss the bus out of Machu Picchu.

I wanted to savour every minute, reckoning this might be the only time I ever see or do this. I didn't want to start panicking and rushing like I was catching the Number 52 back home. "There's still people behind us, they can't leave us all behind. And if they do what's the worst thing that'll happen - we'll just get a taxi, or walk." I had no idea where we were going to in the bus or how far it was but I didn't really care.

Eventually we came to the very outside of Machu Picchu. We passed at the edge of the walls - this was as close as we were going to get to actually going into the ancient city today. It gave a better idea of the size and area, so much bigger than I had expected.

Arriving at the entrance, with turnstiles and a reception area was a jolt back into the present time. Outside buses pulled up and were pulling away. We weren't last and we weren't stranded, there were quite a few other people hanging around in groups. We formed a raggedy queue and then all piled on the next bus. The drive was down a zig zag road that was really nothing but hair pin bends. It was hard to tell if the road was wide enough for two lanes but didn't really matter as the bus stayed more or less in the middle of the road. I assumed there'd be nothing else coming in the opposite direction at this time of night.

It took about 20 minutes or so before we pulled into 'Machu Picchu town' - Aguas Caliente. This place next to one the most visited site in Peru, is a small, unassuming looking town. The Main Street has train tracks running down the middle of it, instead of a road, so you cross looking out for trains rather than cars. The name means hot waters and there are indeed hot springs here too − though our schedule didn't fit it in, I did think a dip in these ones at the end of the trek would have been a welcome idea.

Half way down the main street we crossed over the rail tracks alongside men pushing wheelbarrows full of stones, and gathered in the reception of El President hotel. We went through the by now familiar group rigmarole of sorting out bags, checking in and getting keys. Hot, sweaty and sunburnt I was looking forward to a shower and didn't care if it was cold.

Rose and I were sharing a room on the first floor and after we dumped our bags I walked up to the floor above to see Claire's room. The steps up to the top floor led onto an outside balcony that had the room doors going off it. The view was of rooftops across the small town, mostly flat concrete, some red tiled, some corrugated iron, where washing lines hung from one end to the other. It was a glimpse into life in this little clustered town where low rise buildings jostled close together and the worldwide issue of where do you dry your laundry had to be solved.

Our small room soon filled up - with clothes as we shoved stuff in and out of bags, with steam as we quickly grabbed the hot water before it ran out, and with the unfamiliar smells of cleanliness and perfumes. We had a bit of time before we had to gather together again as per Tony's instructions so Claire, Rose and I decided to look around.

We got only a few metres from the hotel and meandered into an indoor market where we mooched around stalls mostly selling all the same tourist type goodies - t shirts, fridge magnets, bags, hats. I couldn't resist a tiny woollen version of a Peruvian hat - perfect for Squeaky who by now was well and truly one of the gang. By the time we got back into the hotel we'd kept up the tradition of being the last ones to appear.

The restaurant we were heading to was Indio Feliz, Tony explained, owned by the family of an old friend. Originally a French chef, they had met when Tony was a long haired hippy trekking the then distinctly non tourist Inca trail for the first time. "It wasn't like it is now, there weren't people or any facilities. No guides. In fact there wasn't even much of a trail." It was easy to imagine Tony as a young Indiana Jones style adventurer slashing his way through overgrown undergrowth with a machete.

We walked through a square with a statue in the centre and on one side a building that had been developed in keeping with the style of the older stone ones around but was unmistakably modern.

This was the Town Hall, with a couple of police officers were hanging around outside. It was another reminder we were back in 'civilisation'.

There some kind of work being done to the paths - or maybe it was to the road, it was hard to tell as it was pretty much the same thing. The ongoing maintenance to whatever bit of ground it was meant that we had to walk over slightly rickety wooden boards and past temporary hoardings to get to the restaurant. It would have been a little hard to find, disguised by these and tucked away down a side street. It was about a ten minute walk, though everything in the town looked like it would just be a ten minute walk, any further and you'd find you'd actually left it.

We entered a garishly bright interior, green walls with golden accessories, pillars painted orange and murals on every inch of space. We were shown upstairs where a door folded shut so we had our own private room. They must have known we were likely to get very noisy. There was a celebratory buzz in the air, although tomorrow night was officially 'gala night' back in Cusco, everyone seemed to be feeling a sense of achievement and relief and we were ready to let our hair down. Everyone that is except poor Michelle who had Inca two-stepped her way along the final bit of the Inca trail, and decided to give this evening's meal a miss.

I sat with the rest of the original Peak Posse at one table - behind us along the wall stretched three tables that the others all found seats at. As the whole group couldn't all sit together it seemed only right to be with the original group I'd met very first of all.

"I am starving." I declared, quite pleased about it. After feeling not particularly hungry all week, I was now ravenous. The long menu handed to us on large laminated sheets had plenty of vegetarian variety. The babble of conversation was rising as we picked through the menus, a little taken aback by the sheer number of choices.

While we were trying to make up our minds we ordered drinks, most of us having the local beer Cusquena. This arrived ice cold, served in a frosted glass - whether altitude, lack of alcohol, or just because it was really needed, it was undoubtedly the best beer I have ever tasted - pure Inca gold!

Tony's assertion that this was the 'best food around' was totally true - and his recommendations were spot on. In particularly the melon dish he had suggested I have for starters became legendary. It was a scooped out cantaloupe that served as the bowl and was filled - literally filled to the brim - with a red berry liqueur. The melon balls were placed on top but the tastiest part was undoubtedly savouring the liqueur sucked through a straw. It took the longest to get through as well, even though I shared it round. I was in food heaven, especially after days of little desire.

I plumped for 'salmon trout', with a spicy sauce and accompaniment of chillies, which also came with side dishes of sweet potato, gigantic stuffed tomatoes and potato wedges. I then tried to be healthy and went for a liqueur laced fruit salad but looked enviously at Jo's chocolate pudding. It was just as well we'd been segregated from the rest of the diners as not surprisingly the noise levels rose during the meal. Lots of laughter, jokes, stories, cheers and toasts filled the room. Even Tony looked a little relaxed - or maybe just relieved. There was a such a positive atmosphere, everyone in the group was happy and relaxed and I was proud to be part of it.

13 A closer look

'Machu Picchu is sort of like the Inca cosmos written on the landscape.'
Turn Right at Machu Picchu

Friday was our last full day in Peru. It was a day without trekking, which after only four days seemed an odd concept and led to confusion about what to wear. Today we'd be just tourists wandering round with all the other tourists - although there was something about knowing what we'd done to get there that felt like we'd actually earned the right to see Machu Picchu. It was a day without having to plan what gear to put into which bags. Everything was heading back to Cusco with us, so it all just got unceremoniously shoved in wherever it could fit.

We were, as always, up early to be on the first bus back up to Machu Picchu. Though we'd been boisterous and enjoyed our celebratory meal the evening before, we'd been pretty well behaved, too tired for anything else, and had headed straight back to the hotel and bed.

The appetite I'd rediscovered the previous day was still with me and I was again ravenous. I tucked into the buffet breakfast in the hotel with its wonderful weird mix of offerings. Whatever you wanted you'd find it, whether fruit, bread, jams, yoghurt, cheese or meat. The coffee was thick and strong, and now my preferred alternative to coca tea. It felt like some semblance of 'normality' was being restored.

After piling bags in a room downstairs and handing keys in we left the hotel and wandered up the street to the bus stop we'd arrived at yesterday. It felt a little odd not having to have a rucksack full of gear and multitude of all weather clothing. I'd zipped off the bottoms of my trek trousers and was wearing a 'normal' t-shirt with the shorts. Although I still had a small rucksack all it had was my purse, passport and sun cream in it.

Despite the early hour there was already quite a queue at the bus stop when we took our places in it. There was a notice that gave prices for the bus tickets, with variations for adults and children, locals and visitors. As with all elements in this trip we didn't need to know any of that, it was all sorted for us. We just had to turn up and get on. Looking down from the bus stop in the day light, Aguas Calientes was another dramatic setting, settled in a valley with mountains towering around it, complete with river cutting through it as well as the railway track. Despite the amount of visitors that stop here on their way to Machu Picchu and the hotels and obvious nods to tourism, it looked like a small working town that just happened to be next to one of the world's most famous attractions.

We boarded the bus to do the route we'd taken last night in reverse. The skills of all of the drivers we'd experienced were nothing short of incredible. Here they knew the sharp bended road like the back of their hand, navigating with certainty and confidence. When we came to a very sudden halt it was because there was a large snake in the road. The driver hadn't stopped to avoid running it over but rather knew the tourists would want to take a look. Sure enough there was a flurry of photos taken and he patiently waited until everyone sat down again - then carefully drove around it.

We arrived back at the entrance to Machu Picchu with visibility limited by a thick covering of misty cloud. It was already humid and we'd been warned that it would get hotter here than we'd experienced so far.

While we were having a group session of applying sun tan cream Tony took the chance to let us know what the day's itinerary was. At the entrance we were able to get our passports stamped with a special stamp - purely for a memento, we weren't actually entering another country though it may look like another world.

We had arrived as early as possible to make the most of our time there. It turned out that Paco had once worked as a guide on the site so he'd be leading us around and doing a guided tour of as much as we could fit in. We were only spending the morning at the site, after Paco's whistle stop tour we could either stay wandering on our own for a bit longer or get the bus back into Aguas Caliente. We did have to stick to the schedule though and were due to have lunch at a restaurant in the town before then heading back on the train to Ollantaytambo. From there we'd be getting the bus back to Cusco. It sounded like another very packed day and Tony, understandably, was keen to keep us on track with timings as ever.

I had remembered to take my passport and queued to get the slightly smudged inky image of Machu Picchu in it. Once through the turnstiles we followed Paco, unable to see what was in front or to the sides of us thanks to the dense mist. We stopped and gathered on a grassy platform, perching on a low wall. As the sun got higher and hotter the clouds started to melt away and Machu Picchu started to gradually reveal itself.

In front of where we stood the green stepped terraces just disappeared, dropping into the lush green valley below. Wayna Picchu dominated the background, looming up like a large bodyguard. The ruins that surrounded us were easily identifiable as well planned out buildings, walls and walkways. It was easy to visualise what had been here - what was even more amazing than the sights around us was the unknown. How had the Incas in 1450 with very few tools and little equipment, not using so much as a wheel, managed to build such an incredible city in a stunning but not exactly easy to reach location?

There's been restoration work which continues, but even so the fact that so much of the original city survived, in a place well known for earthquakes, floods, landslides and weather related destruction, is largely due to how it was built. Built without mortar or anything to bond the stones, each one was very carefully and precisely cut and fitted tightly together. Incas were experts of this technique called ashlar. In other areas around Peru the strength of Inca buildings can be seen as they are left standing when others have been destroyed by earthquakes or extreme weather.

Sitting so high and remote, with the surrounding mountains protecting it, the city was shielded from the worst of the rain that caused landslides further down the mountains and into the valleys below.

By creating the stepped areas like an agricultural skirt around the buildings, including a drainage system, the Incas were able to grow enough essential crops to sustain the inhabitants. Llamas and alpacas, still roaming freely around the site today, would provide meat and wool, water came from a natural spring. In some ways then a pretty perfect location for sustainability.

Despite the apparent remoteness it seems the city's inhabitants did trade with others near and far. Paco told us that it was likely they grew a lot of coca to sell - which of course is still very much a prized commodity today.

Originally Machu Picchu is thought to have had around 200 buildings and was home to about 1,000 people. After the effort that must have gone into building it, up to 5,000 people could have been involved in the construction, it then appears to have been abandoned after just 100 years. Exactly why it was built and why it was suddenly deserted remain mysteries although many theories abound. Although it's only about 50 miles from Cusco the Spaniards didn't discover it so it wasn't destroyed or plundered like so many other sites.

Hiram Bingham originally thought it was a female dominated home for 'Virgins of the Suns' who worshipped the Inca sun gods.Later examinations of skeletons found at the site showed that around half the population were male and there is little evidence of human sacrificial acts.

Another theory is that Machu Picchu was built because of its 'scared location'. The Incas worshipped the sun and during solstices and equinoxes Machu Picchu aligns precisely with mountains that were religiously significant. It is completed surrounded by the Urubamba, which to the Incas was a sacred river. There is also a stone at Machu Picchu that the Incas believed held the sun in its place along its annual path in the sky.

Yet another viewpoint is that it was built as a royal retreat for the fifteenth century Inca Emperor Pachacuti. And there are several other theories, ranging from suggestions it was built as a prison, to an agricultural testing ground, to claims of it being built by and for aliens.

Part of the intrigue is due to the fact that all of the Incas' history, skills and knowledge were passed down verbally, they didn't use any kind of writing or illustrations, so not written records exist.

The mystery surrounding Machu Picchu is surely part of its attraction though. It is such an intriguing place full of secrets and wonder, that, I hope, we'll never really know for certain all of the answers.

Enthusiastically embracing his role as our expert guide, Paco explained he was going to take us to the key parts of the site, as we wouldn't have time to see all of it. Asking questions and taking photos we moved around, following him. We stopped and gathered round to have explanations of ket points we were at - the temples, the living quarters, the stones that would be filled with water so the Incas could study the stars at night reflected back at them.

The Incas set out Machu Picchu in a determinedly well planned, organised way. Different areas had specific uses - with the site split into agricultural areas, residential zones, parts for temples and worship, a main plaza for everyone to gather in - and even a 'royal' district.

Not surprisingly with their dedication to religion and spiritual practices, there are several sacred areas and temples in the city. One, the Temple of the Sun, is an elliptical design, with a rock inside that is believed to have been an altar. During the June solstice the sun rises and shines directly through one of the temple's windows onto the altar - sun, window and altar in perfect alignment. There is another carved altar found in what's known as the 'main' temple. Another building is known as the Temple of the Three Windows, also dedicated to the sun god - it has three walls as well as three windows, whether on purpose or unfinished is unclear. In here it appears pottery was deliberately thrown and smashed for some reason, fragments can still be found. The Temple of the Condor with its stone-carved shape of the sacred bird's wings may possibly have been used for animal sacrifices. There has never been any evidence found of human sacrifices being carried out at Machu Picchu despite speculation.

Another remaining puzzle is the Intihuatana - a giant rock on a raised platform above the main plaza. The exact purpose of this isn't known. It could, suggest some, have been used for some sort of astronomical observations. Many believe that it was like a sun dial, used for determining the solstices by tracking the sun rays.

This Intihuatana is the now the only one that remains well preserved. Ones that were found by the Spaniards in other Inca cities were damaged or completely destroyed. Some believe that the rock has special powers and they can absorb its energy by putting their hands on it - it is the only thing on the site that is roped off so you can touch though not get any closer to it.

We passed three men, with overalls and caps on, sat on a wall drinking from bottles. In front of them they had tools which looked like gardening trowels. They weren't in any kind of hurry as when we past them later on they were still seemingly on the same tea break. It was difficult to know whether this slow, manual work is due to the nature of the site and restoration, or if it was just 'the way' as we had seen repairs being carried out on the road to Aguas Caliente in a very similar vein.

Having survived for hundreds of years despite extreme weather and invaders, the biggest threat to Machu Picchu now is its popularity. UNESCO has considered putting it on its 'in danger' list. It must be hard to get the balance right. It is a huge attraction that brings in major income not just for the area but for the whole country, yet also needs to be protected and preserved.

Some of the ideas for development in the past are ones that thankfully have never been allowed (yet)- a cable car, tourist complex, luxury hotels – all of which incited protests from academics, scientists and members of the public.

In 2011 the numbers of visitors allowed to enter the site was restricted to 2,500 per day - that's still a whole lot of people. As we moved around throughout the morning it got increasingly busy. The size of our group meant other people had to go around us as we blocked their way, taking up room in the passages and rooms as we crowded together to listen to Paco.

Llamas wandered proprietarily wherever they fancied, with haughty expressions. They didn't respect heritage nor humans - at one point I looked up as I heard a furore, one llama was chasing another and people had to scatter out of their way as they loped past, along the top of ancient walls.

After a while of wandering together we came to a halt and Tony took over the lead. This was as far as our guided tour went. We had to decide whether to catch a bus back to the town now or we could have another half an hour walking around by ourselves - but would have to get the bus back in time for lunch in Aguas Caliente.

Although there was more of Machu Picchu to see and it's easily a place you could keep wandering around, without a guide or guide book I wasn't convinced I'd be able to appreciate any more in just half an hour. I was also tiring and starting to find it quite hard to take in all of the information. If I was going again I thought the best thing would probably be to do it over two days and choose the quietest times - first thing or last thing in the day to spend a few hours each time. It felt a bit of a shame we were rushing back to sit in a restaurant, as it would have been a fantastic day and setting for a picnic lunch.

I headed back to the entrance with the others, on the way passing a plaque dedicated to Hiram Bingham. He is obviously given credit despite being a controversial figure, with some of his exaggerated claims being exposed later by his own son. I guess if you were an olden day explorer it may have been understandable embellishing your adventures in a way not possible today. But his 'discovery' and its publicity must have been a double edged sword for the Peruvian people and government. Not only creating the challenges of preserving one of the world's top tourists attractions but also having had many of the treasures from the site taken out of the country and stored at Yale University in the US. The last of these weren't returned until very recently.

We got the bus back into Aguas Caliente and decide to wander around the market stalls, not knowing whether we'd have much time after lunch. They are towards the railway station, making it impossible to get off the train and not walk through them, perfectly placed for maximum footfall.
It was a riot of colours, with bags, jumpers, ponchos and material galore, and the ubiquitous pens, mugs, fridge magnets. All the stalls were staffed by women, many had children of varying ages with them, from tiny babies to ones that looked school age. It seemed that if there aren't any family members at home to look after them then they just bring the children along.

The prices were already so low, I seemed to have finally got the hang of converting it into English pounds, that to haggle and ask for money off felt mean. I don't like haggling at the best of times so I just paid whatever was asked. I was glad I'd got my cloth from the lady in the mountains, mud and all, as there weren't any in the markets as intricate or unique.

Reckoning that we'd have an hour or two at the most in Cusco the next morning and not wanting to really be rushing round then, this was the only chance for a bit of shopping. I worked out prices much more carefully than usual, given my financially precarious status due to my hospital bill. This was probably a good thing as I'd probably have bought a lot more just for the sake of bringing back 'bargains' - alpaca wool jumpers, cardigans, scarves, hats, socks, woven handbags, rucksacks, hippy bags, silver earrings, necklaces, rings. I plumped for some top tourist tat for Dylan including a lime green Inca Kola t-shirt, a scarf that I was assured was 'best alpaca' for my mum, and woolly hat complete with little llama figures on it for my brother. I wanted to save some money as was determined to at least get to the chocolate museum the next day.

We trooped into a modern, shiny restaurant almost opposite the hotel for lunch. I felt particularly scruffy, turning up to somewhere quite so clean in dirty hiking boots and mud spattered shorts. I reckoned I was going to be happy leaving trekker chic behind. The staff were friendly and of course our guides well known to them, wherever we went we did get excellent service and lots of attention. There was a jovial, relaxed atmosphere and after we ordered, delicious smells start to fill the room.

There was a television on the wall with adverts being shown for London. Paco told us it was his dream to visit England and asked us about where we lived. We worked out that if he came to stay with each of us in turn he could pretty much cover all parts of the country. The lunch was another delicious three course indulgence, I was so pleased I was enjoying the food again. Paco, as was now tradition, finished off anything that anyone was going to leave.

Afterwards there was a slow meander back through the markets and to the train station for the return journey. Still never able to miss an opportunity to try out a toilet, a few of us visited the ones in the station. They were not just clean - they had doors, seats, and toilet paper, and flushed properly. I reckoned it would definitely give people the wrong impression if that was their first toilet experience in Peru.

On the train we sat in allocated seats, spread throughout in the carriage. Unlike the first journey, when we buzzed with the excitement of getting here, the mood was quieter, chat died down and people start to nod off. I mused on the fact that we'd come all this way, trekked for four days, had a few hours at Machu Picchu then it seemed we were very suddenly on our way back. It felt slightly unreal, as if we were just heading for our next stop, not starting the long journey home. Tony was one of the ones getting a nap in, having taken himself further down the carriage, quite probably for some peace and quiet. I imagined he'd be quite relieved when he finally waved us all off and he could actually start to relax.

We arrived back at Ollyantambo and said goodbye to Inca Rail later in the afternoon. There was a short walk from the train station to an area where cars and buses were parked - but when we arrived, ours wasn't in sight. Paco and Tony looked around, had a discussion, then there was a flurry of phone calls. They reported back - our bus had broken down somewhere and they were trying to get another one sorted. Tony's worried face returned, concerned about getting back in time to get to the restaurant.

The biggest worry in the group wasn't about missing out on a meal but about not having time to change and get make up and hair done. After watching most of the other vehicles depart and consideration of how many taxis we may need if it came to it, eventually our bus showed up. Now feeling quite weary, I climbed aboard, heading back to Cusco.

14 Gala night

'Let us celebrate the occasion with wine and sweet words.' Plautus

It was the least worrying, most comfortable bus journey we experienced in Peru. On the way back to Cusco on board the biggest concern among the group was whether we'd have enough time to get changed not just for the meal but for a 'proper' night out. This was 'Gala Night' as it was termed in the itinerary.

Although a couple of the girls had miraculously managed to stay looking quite glamorous even in the most dire environments, most of us were looking forward to scrubbing up a bit - with fresh clothes, make up, hair done, the works. Tony was insistent that the time booked for the meal couldn't be changed, we couldn't be any later, so rotas were being drawn up for shared use of showers, hair dryers and straighteners.

Our route back to Cusco took in stunning scenery, the vast mountains consistently dominated the view, looming over the towns settled at the bottom of them, pointing into the clear sky. Tony pointed out parts that we'd been near to, it was odd to think we had been up so high on something that looked so impressive and intimidating.

We were going through small towns with low buildings, market stalls, occasional cars, passing signs of communities. We stopped outside a hotel, the front of it, right on the dusty road, looked unassuming. Our lovely lady doctor was getting off here and joining another group and we said fond farewells.

As the stars started to pop on like fairy lights, we reached a recognisable plateau with the huge Jesus statue. A cheer erupted and the bus headed down as we had our first sight of Cusco again huddling at the bottom of the valley. As ever, it took longer than it looked to reach the lights and buildings we could see from the top but after zig zagging our way down we finally hit a flat road. We were back.

The streets became more familiar looking and we were in tired but high spirits by the time we piled back into the same hotel we'd left just a few days but a whole experience ago. Our bags were once again there waiting for us, magically appearing as they had done all week. There was the usual noisy chaos as we collected our belongings and sorted out who was in which room. Myself, Claire and Rose were shown to a three bed one on the first floor. I suddenly slowed down as I went up the stairs, feeling 'that altitude' again.

We didn't see any other guests at the hotel but if there were any they may well have been disturbed by shouts through the walls, knocking on doors and the general kerfuffle that is the result of 15 females being given just over half an hour to get ready for a night out.

In our room I flinched as I pulled clothes out of my bags. There was an overwhelming damp, musty, mouldy smell coming from the trekking stuff that had never had a chance to dry out and had been festering, creating an increasingly powerful aroma. I piled it all into plastic bags and knotted the tops tightly, hoping that these would be somehow air tight enough to also be smell tight.

There was very little time and we negotiated turns in the shower and use of the non too powerful electric socket. By the time we were ready, it looked an explosion had scattered the entire contents of our bags across every single surface of the room.

Complete with Squeaky in his new hat and his new pal Paddington Bear (who'd been travelling with Jo) our freshly showered, cleaned up, dressed up, hair styled group headed off in a perfumed cloud down the street towards the main square.

It was our last night - the gala night that had been billed as the chance to celebrate and finally let our hair down, after an exhilarating but exhausting week. Tomorrow rather than wake at the crack of dawn and prepare for a day's walking, all we had to do was pack and face the return trip home.

We were all excited - but there was one person who must've been looking forward to it even more. For Tony, who had looked after us all so well all week, fussed and fretted with fatherly concern, smiled even when we must have been testing his patience, kept us all on track and got us back safe and sound, it must have been a relief. More than that though, tonight we were going to be joined by his very own 'Chi-chi', his wife of over 30 years. You could feel their affection and love from the way he talked about her, his eyes brightened and it was always with a smile. We knew he didn't like being apart from her for too long and he was looking forward to being reunited with her. We were all curious and keen to meet her too.

The restaurant we were going to was La Retama, which overlooked the main square. We were led up a flight of stairs, into a bright room, past a buffet table loaded with food and shown to a long table where we took our seats.

Tony's face lit up as a dark haired lady approached - it had to be Chichi. Friendly, warm and welcoming she was as smiley and twinkly as Tony was and came round to introduce herself and have a chat with us.

We were in a large L shaped room, with music coming from a small Peruvian group in the middle of it, all ponchos, tall hats and pan pipes. It was definitely going to be a night to embrace local tradition - the meat eaters in the group had all decided to club together and order a roast guinea pig so they could at least have a taste - when in Peru and all that...

We'd helped ourselves to a selection from the buffet meal, with many of the vegetarian options being potato related, by the time something resembling a charred skinned rat was brought out. With great ceremony, and I am sure a glint in the waiter's eye, it was deposited in the middle of the table. Lying prone on a large silver platter it looked like it had just been cooked where it died - it was complete with head, limbs and claws. A giant sized chilli pepper stuffed into its mouth 'to shut it up' completed its undignified look.

There are times when, as a vegetarian, I get a craving for something carnivorous, usually tempted by a gorgeous smell or sight of a meaty dish. But this was definitely not one of those times. This dish could easily have the opposite effect and increase the ranks of non meat eaters judging by the faces pulled as it appeared.

Small bits were carved off, it didn't look like it would stretch to filling a whole plate for one anyway, not being the meatiest looking creature. The plates were passed around, with us vegetarians looking on curious but, given the reactions, happy not to be trying it. 'Doesn't really taste of anything' - 'maybe a bit like pork' - 'hmmmmm' - were some of the reactions. The biggest 'yuck' was saved for one girl who on her plate got a full paw complete with claw as her taster.

Having had the obligatory pisco sours we were mostly drinking wine, not sure of what it was except not Peruvian, but it went down well. Having been very sensible all week, if not by choice but by altitude, the Inca Two Step and general exhaustion, everyone seemed to be embracing the party spirit for our grand finale. The Peruvian band started playing recognisable tunes and suddenly our table burst into song, singing along to the best of the Beatles tunes played on panpipes.

The restaurant was busy and the tables around us had filled up. In one corner we heard a group of men debating whether to have the guinea pig, they were young, possibly gap year-ers, definitely British. When their dark brown rodent appeared squeaking noises came from our table, reaching a crescendo as they hesitatingly took bites from their meal, glancing over, obviously wanting to keep up their bravado.

Tonight was also awards night. This was a not too secret secret - as at the airport Claire had been handed a heavy package and tasked with looking after the medals. She had also been asked by the guides to write something suitable they could say about each of the group on the day she had been in Aguas Caliente without us.

Tony and Paco called for hush and stood at the head of the table, medals and notes in hand. One by one they read out a precis with highlights of each person's journey, traits and observations and one by one we got up to get a medal and hug from each of them to applause from the others. At the end it was their turn, and they were given our views and highlights - the many toilet stops, reminding Paco to say por favour, constantly upsetting Tony's strict timetable, putting up with our tendency to find anything remotely hilarious, - and our thanks - for looking after us, motivating us, making what was a difficult challenge also so much fun, keeping our spirits up, and getting us there.

When they said that we were the best group they had led, we believed them, not least as we could see tears in their eyes (though these could of course have just been tears of joy and relief...)

We talked about everyone's highlights of the trip, toasting each one, then raised another glass when Rose reminded us of the reason we were doing this at the end of the day. We worked out that between us we had raised around £50,000 for Breast Cancer Care.

There were more cheers and toasts at this.

The band struck up again, now playing salsa tunes, Claire, who had learned to salsa and was very good at it and Michelle, who hadn't had lessons but had bags of enthusiasm, led the way dancing in front of the band. One by one more people got up and joined in from our group, most of the other diners had gone then and we were soon the only ones left in the restaurant.

When it was time for the musicians to leave, a sound system was turned on and the night turned into scenes of dancing a mix of disco and salsa. After the restaurant's usual closing time, Tony persuaded them to stay open for us, the wine kept flowing and music kept going, with the staff and waiters joining in.

Eventually and not before there'd been a fair share of typical Friday night out tears, cheers, and drunken conversations, the same as you get anywhere in the world, Tony decided we really did have to go and let them close up the restaurant. He managed to herd us outside, where someone immediately spotted something that was still open and loud next door. It was a 'proper' disco and as some of the group disappeared up the stairs, Tony started to try to tell them that it was really not a good idea. His advice fell on deaf ears and he was only stopped going in to accompany them by being persuaded that they really were old enough to look after themselves. Tonight they weren't his responsibility, they promised they would stay in a group and all come back to the hotel together.

Reluctant as he was, he agreed he'd leave them to it, but still worrying to the last. Though I'd been tempted to join them I knew in the morning I'd be glad I resisted. Instead I wound my way back to the hotel with the others and immediately sank into a deep sleep as soon as my head hit the pillow.

15 The Morning After

'I used to want the words 'She tried' on my tombstone. Now I want 'She did it." Katherine Dunham

I woke up relatively early, given that it had been about 1am when we'd finally made it back. I looked around the room. Claire had been among the nightclubbers and I was glad to see she was back safely. No matter how quiet the first one to stir was we seemed to have a naturally synchronised waking up mechanism and Rose and Claire both murmured as I slowly sat up.

Claire filled us in on the night club where they'd danced and, as Tony had instructed them, kept all together and kept hold of their handbags. We exchanged notes on the night, filling in gaps of each other's memories or conversations we'd missed while we'd been too busy dancing or talking to someone else.

We all moved carefully around the room coordinating bathroom trips. There was still a schedule to keep of course. We had until about noon free to do our own thing but needed to get ready, pack and prepare for our journey back before going anywhere. First things first though - strong coffee was needed. We went to the breakfast room where some of the others were already comparing hangovers and flashbacks. Not sure if eating was a good idea or not I stuck to a just having a bit of bread but the fresh orange juice and coffee were really welcome. Everyone had made it back to the hotel safely last night though Suzanne came in with a concerned look on her face. Andrea had slipped and bumped her head going for a shower. She wasn't feeling too good so had gone back to bed for a lie down.

There were sympathetic noises and general agreement that she'd probably feel fine after a sleep. Nobody had any particular plans, except to finish packing then mooch around. By the time we headed back to our room it was already about 9am. I realised I was really wasn't going to get to see Cusco at all. A week ago I'd have probably wanted to go and spend some time on my own looking around but staying together with Claire and Rose, especially with a slightly tender head, just seemed like the natural thing to do. "The only thing I definitely want to do is go to the chocolate museum, " I said. They were in agreement, not least because it was easy to find, just down the street from the hotel - and they served coffee and hot chocolate.

First we had to tackle the packing. I was unsure how, although i hadn't really bought a lot extra, I was going to get everything back into my one large rucksack. The answer was to spread everything out on the floor, leave a lot of stuff behind, and pack the rucksack as tightly as possible, wrapping the still stinking trek items tightly inside two bin bags.

I had no idea why I'd brought the bin bags except they were on the kit list but I was now grateful for them. I tied the tops as tight as possible to hopefully keep the smell in. Heaven help any airport security person who asked to see inside that lot. Despite my woolly head I remembered that if I was to take Dylan Inca Kola back as I'd promised it'd have to go into the hold luggage.

I wrapped the sleeping bag round it and prayed the plastic bottles wouldn't smash. I'd hired the sleeping bag and didn't fancy trying to clean the sticky sweet gloop out of it before I sent it back.

We debated what to leave behind. There were hardly used toiletries and not used at all antiseptic hand gels that I'd left behind in the bag at the hotel - they could definitely stay. I had lots of foot and blister stuff I'd never used because the one thing I hadn't had any trouble with were my feet. We hadn't walked far or fast enough to get blisters really and my boots had been surprisingly comfortable. I found water sterilisation tablets, also unused, and recalled the man in the outdoor shop when I bought them telling me they'd be a waste of money as 'everyone gets the squits trekking up there'. How right he was. We were now debating about leaving any trekking gear, in particular our boots.

"Well,' I said. "I definitely won't be trekking again but I'll take them home as they're good for long walks with the dog."

By the time we were sorted and ready to take our bags down the stairs there were various items piled up on the beds. A lot was too good to throw away but I guessed someone else would get use out of them.

The three of us meandered out of the hotel entrance and down the street towards the Chocolate Museum, everyone else going their own way in pairs or small groups. It took just a few minutes to reach the sign and we walked through an archway that opened out into a square courtyard. I wished I'd had more time to explore Cusco as guessed I'd find much more to see hidden away down the little alley ways and tucked behind the main streets.

We followed the signs up a wooden flight of stairs and as we came out onto the balcony we were greeted by the most wonderful welcoming, mouth watering aroma. We had arrived at undoubtedly the best smelling museum I had ever been to - Choco Museo. Once through the double doors we were greeted by smiling people wearing pristine aprons and even stronger chocolate smells - it was like sticking your face into a bowl full of dark chocolate powder and just breathing it in. You could taste the air.

It was clear that it was less like a museum and more a working chocolatier. There were pictures and diagrams and information on the wall from which I found out that there is a push to replace coca growing with cocoa - just one letter but a world of difference. There was plenty to look at and to buy, and we were able to look into the rooms at the heart of the Museo to see the chocolate action going on. You can book onto workshops and classes. Further back were a few tables and chairs and we agreed that our next move should be to sit and taste some of the goods. We moved to the small balcony and found it was the perfect size for a table and three chairs.

We ordered drinks and sat, grateful for the rest even though we had hardly walked any distance, the tiredness, altitude and hangover mix was definitely kicking in.

The balcony overlooked the main square, we could see all around for miles as most building were no higher than one storey. In front of us the cathedral dominated the plaza and further on was the road where Cusco met the mountains and we'd travelled up towards Jesus on the hill.

We sat in the sunshine, this I thought, is what I have missed. It was the first time I had just been able to sit, relax, people watch and just breathe the place in. I knew I would really like to come back to Cusco to get to know it, and the rest of the Sacred Valley – as well as the rest of Peru.

The drinks arrived, we'd ordered various coffees and they came with - what else - complimentary chocolates. The flavours of both were intense and quality. As we sipped and passed comments on the goings on in the square we could see some of our group wandering about, others sitting at a cafe at the other side. We waved across at each other.

Suddenly a flat bed truck with a police sign flew up the road and screeched to a halt. Half a dozen uniformed policemen who'd been balancing in the back jumped down. One of them ran across the road and tackled a women who dropped a bag she was carrying. Arms locked behind her back she was frog marched into the jeep, they all got back on board and drove off. We sat gaping at the scene, but it seemed to have had little impact on anyone else in the street. Her bag was left where it had fallen, people just wandered past seemingly unperturbed. We finished our drinks and quite reluctantly agreed we really should move- the one thing that was a 'must do' was for Rose to get a piece of jewellery to take home for her daughter.

We stopped in the shop near the entrance of the museum and stocked up on chocolate related items to take back as gifts. It seemed you could make just about anything and I bought some chocolate tea for Dylan that didn't really look like either chocolate or tea and samples of dark chocolate which when I got home were given the seal of approval by chocolate loving friends as the 'best ever tasted.'

We walked across the square towards stalls and shop fronts and paused at the cafe some of the others were sitting in. Suzanne told us that Andrea had been sick and was still feeling rough, so had stayed at the hotel. With the long journey ahead we all hoped she'd be feeling better by the time we had to leave.

We meandered slowly in and out of various shops. There was a huge choice of gorgeous jewellery and it took a while to decide on exactly what but when she did Rose haggled, as we'd been advised, for a necklace and earrings. I was as impressed as she was.

As we wandered across the square, stopping to take photos, a man stopped, smiling. It was one of the waiters from the restaurant we'd been in. He was on his way back to work and stopped to say hello. As he did we heard a shout and looked up. Another man was opening the restaurant, leaning over the balcony and waving at us. It was a reminder of what a small place this really was, and how friendly. I felt it would be a pretty safe place to come as a solo traveller even if you hadn't done anything too adventurous before.

We decided we had done all of the walking around we felt up to and the best thing to do would be to get some lunch before it was time to head back to the hotel to set off. If the return journey was anything like the one getting there it would be a long while until we saw proper food again.

We wandered up one of the streets that led off from the square. There were quite a few cafes, most of them you had to go inside as there wasn't really room in this narrow cobbled street to have tables outside. We pushed a door open and went upstairs to what looked like an empty bar at the top. A menu on the door showed faded photos of burgers, chips, sandwiches. It looked like it would do the job - post night out stodge to kick the hangover into touch and keep us going. We walked through the room saying hello to a man behind the bar and the waitress in front of it. Other than that it was empty though understandably as it was still a bit early for lunch. The smiling waitress waved her hands at a lot of empty tables - and we chose our spot on another balcony.

We decided to share a couple of plates of chips and sandwiches - such a change after all the fabulous dishes we'd had made for us throughout the week. I looked around. We were high enough to see the missing slates on the roofs opposite. It also looked as if someone was trying to rig up their own electricity off someone else's power, cables were slung in a gung-ho fashion from one building to the next, different sizes and colours, some taped together.

It seemed to take a long time for our basic fare to arrive, although a few others had come in by then it was by no means busy. We decided it was just 'the way', why would you rush - if we didn't have a bus and then a plane to catch I would quite easily and very happily sit here all day. When it did arrive it was fresh and fabulous-fat homemade chips and huge wedges of the delicious sweet bread.

We ate in a hurry, conscious now that time was getting on and we were undoubtedly going to be the last ones back at the hotel. I left the last of my sols towards the bill and we headed down. Out in the square I looked around wanting to take it all in for one last time, but we didn't have time to loiter. As we started to climb up the sloping street to the hotel, we commented on the fact there was an paramedic car parked towards the top of it. "That's not for us is it?" we joked.

We got to the hotel, slightly breathless due to the pace we'd walked. The paramedic car was parked right outside the hotel. As we entered, the rest of the group were sat around in the courtyard. We started to apologise for being late then stopped as we saw the expressions on their faces. "It's Andrea," someone said. "She's being taken to hospital."

16 Back to Normal

'It is a strange thing to come home. While yet on the journey, you cannot at all realise how strange it will be.' Selma Lagerl

I suddenly noticed Suzanne, sitting in tears. Andrea was being taken in the ambulance car with a doctor, Suzanne and Paco were going to get a cab to the hospital.

A doctor had been called after Andrea had been sick and as she'd bumped her head they didn't want to take any chances. They wanted to take her for an x-ray and admit her to hospital until they were sure she would be okay to fly. Suzanne was going to stay with her but was understandably upset and worried about them both being left behind. We comforted her as best we could, Tony and Paco both reassuring that they would be with them and they weren't going to leave them alone to deal with things.

Tony looked more stressed than he had all week and I felt sorry for him too. He had started to relax a bit last night and must have been looking forward to getting us all homeward bound today so he could breathe a sigh of relief. But not now.

"The bus is here we really do have to go, we have to get everyone else to the airport on time," he said. Suzanne tried to smile, wiping her eyes and told us all to go and get on the bus. There was little else we could do.

It was a subdued trip to the airport and a rushed goodbye to Tony as we checked in and he dashed back to resume his duties at the hospital with Andrea and Suzanne. All we could do was text Suzanne to let her know we were thinking of them both and for her to keep in touch with any news.

Leaving two of the group behind, two that I'd become good friends with, felt awful. At least there was some comfort in that they were staying together. It was a bizarre, unexpected turn of events - and I am sure pretty unusual for a trip to start off with someone in hospital and then end in the same way.

The flights back were all on time with the long flight from Lima on the same airline with the same surly staff as the one we'd arrived on. Despite feeling exhausted, I found it difficult to sleep and had plenty of time to reflect. It seemed that it had been such a short time that had gone so quickly. Of the ten day trip we'd only spent a week in Peru, the other three days were travelling time.

In some ways it felt longer as it was such an intense week. It had definitely been about a whole new experience unlike anything I've ever had. After four days getting there we'd spent a relatively short amount of time actually at Machu Picchu. It had been, as they say, all about the journey not the destination, the mix of highs and lows, the scary bits and funny parts.

I knew I'd made some good friends that I'd stay in touch with, going through such an experience in such a short time means you get to know people better than you probably do under normal circumstances. This kind of trip is definitely no place to try to keep anything hidden or be anyone different to your real self. Not withstanding the layers of clothes, it kind of stripped everything back.

I knew I'd definitely like to go back to Peru to experience more of the country and also a good deal more time exploring the parts we had been to - especially Cusco and the Sacred Valley.

I'd started off feeling like I'd failed at the first hurdle, being the one needing hospital treatment, who couldn't cope despite all the preparation and fitness training. But actually, I decided, what I should be doing is recognise that as I was so affected it was even more of a challenge, but one I did complete and get through. Why give myself a hard time about that?

The other struggle for me was always going to be being part of a group for so long, but it had been fascinating to discover the different characters and motivations and stories for doing this. There were definite benefits of not having to be responsible for organising everything, keeping things on track and sorting things out if they went wrong, undoubtedly. It was funny how quickly and easily I had got used to not having to cook, not having to think about where I was going or what to do next at any given time.

I had missed not having space and time to be able to my own thing. The altitude, tiredness and busy schedule left very little opportunity just to sit and think let along write about anything. It was though undoubtedly an adventure and experience of a lifetime. I was extremely happy and proud to have done it. It was something I was unlikely to repeat. This was definitely a one off, I couldn't see myself doing a trip like this again.

As we waited at Lima and Madrid airports we kept in contact with and got updates from Suzanne. They had taken X-rays and seemed to think there wasn't anything to worry about but were still going to keep Andrea in overnight as a precaution. She'd contacted their families back home and they would get flights arranged as soon as they could. It was a relief and good news to end the trip on.

It was a tired, raggedy group that arrived at Heathrow - now focused on the last individual leg of the journey, we had an array of more planes, trains or cars to get. Understandably we were all also now talking about seeing our families, impatient to see them again. We said goodbyes around the luggage reclaim area and people drifted off as the bags came out at differing times.

Myself and Mel then had to go for our last leg - the final plane back to Newcastle. We'd flown over 5,000 miles to get this far but this short domestic flight was the one that was delayed – of course.

As we waited, worn out and just wanting to get home, another fleece wearing lady spotted a Charity Challenge tag and started talking to us. She was just back from another trek organised by them - she'd been for a week out in the Sahara. It was her third trek with Charity Challenge, she told us and she was already planning the next one. "You'll get addicted to them," she said. 'Once you've done one, I bet you'll end up doing more." I reassured her that, amazing as it had been, one was enough for me, 'never again'.

Finally we were on the plane and heading home. I wanted to put a sign around my neck declaring that I had been on a trek, had camped out in the Andes, hadn't had a really hot shower or washed my hair properly for a week. I felt very alien sitting surrounded by people wearing smart suits and normal clothes, carrying hand bags and lap tops.

     I knew that Dylan and my dad were coming to meet me and I couldn't wait to see them. I started feeling impatient at the baggage collection, quickly picked up my bags and headed through the doors. It felt like both a lifetime and no time at all since I'd stood there and said goodbye to my son. I saw him as I walked through the exit, big grins spread across both our faces and as we met I hugged him harder than ever.

***

It took a while to adjust after the trek. Not only to get rid of the jet lag and exhaustion but to get back into 'normality'. In the days afterwards I took the dog to the beach and it didn't feel normal stopping after just half an hour, I wanted to carry on just walking. It didn't feel normal going to a crowded shopping centre and seeing people spending their time and lots of money on just buying 'stuff'. Having to not just decide what to eat but then also cook it for myself wasn't normal. Having to take responsibility for myself and others, even though I like it that way, didn't feel normal for a while. Being on my own, with all the time, space and solitude I'd craved wasn't normal. I missed my girlfriends, I missed giggling with the others on a daily, if not hourly, basis. I missed having to think about nothing more serious than which item to put into which bag. I missed the open spaces, the incredible landscape, the awe inspiring mountains. I missed Tony and Paco. I missed heading into the unknown each day.

Some months later I was at home when Claire rang. After we exchanged pleasantries and updates when she revealed her real reason for ringing.

"You know it's my 50th birthday next year?"

"Yes."

"Well, I want to do something special. I'm going to do another Charity Challenge trek."

"Really?" I guessed what might be coming next. "Where?"

"Cuba. It's trekking through the Escambray mountains in Cuba. What do you think? Are you up for it? Come with me?"

I hesitated for just a moment, recalling my previous vow of 'never again'.

"Yes. Definitely. I'm in."

Appendices

The Inca Trails

While many people speak of 'the' Inca Trail, the Incas actually built a highly advanced network of nearly 40,000 km of trails connecting their vast empire that stretched throughout South America. Cusco was at the heart of this empire.

A particularly beautiful 43km section of mountain trail connecting important Inca archaeological sites of Runcuracay, Sayacmarca, Phuyupatamarca, Wiñay Wayna and Machu Picchu has become increasingly popular with trekkers over the last 30 years and this is what has become known as 'the Inca Trail to Machu Picchu' - or the classic Inca Trail.

There are alternative Inca Trails and the one that is highlighted in this book is the Lares trek. The Lares Valley lies in the east of the Urupampa mountain range. Lares Valley is home to traditional weavers and farmers many of whom only speak Quechuan and maintain a way of life unchanged in hundreds of years. This trek is at higher altitude than the classic Inca Trail and through a more remote, less visited area.

Access to the classic Inca Trail is now strictly controlled and a limited number of trekking permits are issued - only 500 per day, and of those just 200 are visitors, the rest are guides and porter. If you want to go on this trail it's recommended to book as far in advance of your trip as possible, you'll need to plan certainly several months in advance. June, July and August are high season and this trail is closed during February for conservation work. January and March are rainy season so best avoided.

The Classic Inca Trail to Machu Picchu usually takes four days to complete but shorter treks along the same route are also offered by companies.

Increasingly, especially since the numbers became restricted, alternative Inca Trail treks are becoming more popular. These include the Lares Valley Trail and the Salkantay Trek.

Book your trek with a responsible tour company, one that looks after both the environment and the porters who will be invaluable on your trek.

Other ways to Machu Picchu

If you aren't trekking an Inca Trail you will find that local tour companies will be able to still help you with transport and entrance to Machu Picchu.

If you prefer to arrange your own trip, then the best thing to remember is to book in advance as far as possible. Remember that Aguas Caliente is 'Machu Picchu town' but when you reach there you still have a 20 minute bus journey or an hour's steep uphill hike to get to the site.

Trains

You can get a train from Cusco (Poroy station) to Machu Picchu (Aguas Caliente) - only a few are direct so you may need to change at Ollantaytambo. A direct train takes about three hours. You can find more information and book on www.perurail.com

Inca Rail runs several trains a day from Ollantaytambo to Aguas Calientes, starting at 6.40am this journey takes around one hour and 20 minutes. Information and bookings at www.incarail.com

Aguas Caliente to Machu Picchu

The best way to get to Machu Picchu from the town is by bus. They are very regular - the first one leaves at 5.30am and they then run every 15 minutes throughout the day. The return journey is the same frequency and the last bus leaves Machu Picchu at 5.30pm.

Bus tickets can be bought at the bus station in Aguas Caliente, in some hotels and tourist centres, or in advance. Again, it is advisable to at least buy a ticket the night before as queues grow quickly and people board on a first come first served basis. More information about the bus service is on www.consettur.com

The bus stop is about 200 metres from the train station.

You can go on foot to the site but it is a very steep climb and likely to take around an hour.

Getting into Machu Picchu

You cannot buy tickets into Machu Picchu at the entrance so must get your ticket in advance. If you aren't booking through a tour company or guide you can book through the government run website **www.machupicchu.gob.pe** or commercial agency such as **ticket-machupicchu.com**

Tickets to go up Wayna Picchu are limited to 200 a day and must also be booked in advance - this is separate to your ticket into Machu Picchu.

You must take your passport with you to get into the entrance. You will find there are local guides at the site you can book if you decide you want someone to show you around when you get there.

Only small back packs are allowed into the site - storage is available near the entrance for larger items.

The only toilets are near the entrance - once inside you can be a good 30 minutes away from these so be prepared!

There is only one snack bar so take your own food and drinks - make sure you take water, sun screen and a hat with you as it can get very hot.

References and further information

Charity Challenge is the world's leading fundraising challenge operator. They organise over 100 expeditions each year - including treks, cycle rides, mountain climbs, rafting, dog sledding - and have helped thousands of people raise over £40m for over 1500 different charities.

More information on www.charitychallenge.com

Breast Cancer Care is a charity that supports anyone affected by breast cancer. They provide information and support and campaign for improved standards of care. Around 55,000 people in the UK are diagnosed with breast cancer each year.

www.breastcancercare.org

Cuzco & the Inca Heartland - Footprint Travel Guide
Full Circle - Michael Palin
Turn Left at Machu Picchu - Mark Adams
www.nationalgeographic.com
www.sacredvalleyproject.com
www.peru-facts.co.uk
www.quechuabenefit.com

Accommodation and restaurants

www.hotelesgarcilaso.com
www.hotelsolperu.com
www.hostalpresidente.com
www.indiofeliz.com
www.laretamarestaurant.com

Acknowledgements

I would like to say thank you to everyone who supported me in any way through the fundraising and preparation for this challenge - from helping me raise money for such a good cause to those who listened to me banging on about the lack of toilets and need for wet wipes.

A particular mention of course to the Peru Posse because it wouldn't have been the same without any one of you - Rose, Michelle, Jo, Andrea, Suzanne, Mel, Louise, Sally, Claire A, Linzi, Claire M, Faye, Jane, Lily. I hope my recollection isn't too wide of the mark and it brings back as many good memories for you too. Thank you for getting me through the tough moments and making me laugh so much.

Big thanks and huge respect to Tony and Paco - a brave pair who took on an all female group and survived to tell the tale. Thank you for your encouragement, support, kindness, for sharing your knowledge and passion for your beautiful country, and above all for laughing with us and having such a great sense of humour.

Thanks as always to my mum and dad for being there, holding the fort and just letting me do my own thing as always.

Finally - thank you Dylan, for being supportive of whatever crazy ideas I have, for being the best son I could ever with for, for being insanely great. There is no reason not to follow your heart.

Printed in Great Britain
by Amazon